GETTING OVER NEW LABOUR

Building Progressive Alternatives
Series Editors: David Coates†, Ben Rosamond and Matthew Watson

Bringing *together* economists, political economists and other social scientists, this series offers pathways to a coherent, credible and progressive economic growth strategy which, when accompanied by an associated set of wider public policies, can inspire and underpin the revival of a successful centre-left politics in advanced capitalist societies.

Published

Corbynism in Perspective: The Labour Party under Jeremy Corbyn
Edited by Andrew S. Roe-Crines

Divided They Fell: Crisis and the Collapse of Europe's Centre-Left
Sean McDaniel

The European Social Question: Tackling Key Controversies
Amandine Crespy

Flawed Capitalism: The Anglo-American Condition and its Resolution
David Coates

Getting Over New Labour: The Party After Blair and Brown
Karl Pike

The Political Economy of Industrial Strategy in the UK: From Productivity Problems to Development Dilemmas
Edited by Craig Berry, Julie Froud and Tom Barker

Pursuing the Knowledge Economy: A Sympathetic History of High-Skill, High-Wage Hubris
Nick O'Donovan

Race and the Undeserving Poor: From Abolition to Brexit
Robbie Shilliam

Reflections on the Future of the Left
Edited by David Coates

GETTING OVER NEW LABOUR
The Party After Blair and Brown

KARL PIKE

agenda
publishing

© Karl Pike 2024

First published in 2024 by Agenda Publishing

Agenda Publishing Limited
PO Box 185
Newcastle upon Tyne
NE20 2DH
www.agendapub.com

ISBN 978-1-78821-677-7 (hardcover)
ISBN 978-1-78821-720-0 (paperback)

British Library Cataloguing-in-Publication Data
A catalogue record for this book is available from the British Library

Typeset by JS Typesetting Ltd, Porthcawl, Mid Glamorgan
Printed and bound in the UK by CPI Group (UK) Ltd, Croydon, CR0 4YY

CONTENTS

PREFACE

I have thought about the Labour Party, most days, for over 15 years now. That is not quite as uninteresting as it sounds, I hope. In 2007, I began working for the Labour Party, then became a parliamentary researcher for a Labour MP, and then a political advisor to members of the shadow cabinet. After that, I completed a PhD and became an academic, and my thesis was on Labour in the 1980s and 1990s. Politics is in the news a lot, and I while I mostly enjoy reading about it and hearing people talk about it, I also think it's incredibly important to engage with regardless. So, when you add up the jobs, the experiences, the fascination with politics and the thinking it is important, Labour politics is on my mind at some point, most days, and for good reason I think.

This book is a new take on a political party and a moment in time. The way we look at things is shaped by a great deal, and my beliefs about the Labour Party, and politics more generally, have changed over the years. They will, I am sure, change again. One of the joys of research is discovering different ways of understanding something, affecting your own ways of seeing and thinking. For having made it to this point, many thanks are owed. First, thank you to the MPs I worked with and the Labour Party members I have learnt from over many years. Second, since becoming an academic many colleagues have been incredibly generous with their time and taught me so much. Thank you, in particular, to Peter Allen, Tim Bale (with additional thanks for being a fantastic mentor), Phil Cowley, Madeleine Davis, Patrick Diamond, Nick Garland, Eunice Goes, Farah Hussain, Andrew Hindmoor, Ben Jackson and Colm Murphy. And thanks to colleagues who organize and attend TheoryLab at the School of Politics and International Relations (SPIR) at Queen Mary University of London, as well as my colleagues at the Mile End Institute, also at Queen Mary. While the support of colleagues has undoubtedly made this a better book, any errors are, of course, mine and mine alone.

Special thanks to David Williams, who was the head of SPIR when I was writing this book and was unfailingly supportive; and to Alison Howson, her colleagues at Agenda and those who kindly reviewed the proposal and manuscript for this book. The biggest thanks are owed to Kiran Mahil, Millie Pike and Zadie Pike: all heroes.

INTRODUCTION

Vociferous ambiguity

Philip Gould, Lord Gould of Brookwood, knew the ins and outs of New Labour better than most. When he wasn't writing and sending off memos about public opinion and political strategy, he was in meetings or on the phone with the main players. This filled a lot of his time, from the 1980s to the 2010 general election. Shortly before he died of cancer in November 2011, an updated and expanded edition of his book, *The Unfinished Revolution*, was published. The book had long held cult status among supporters of New Labour, having first been published after New Labour's 1997 election landslide. It had at least one admiring foe, too: the Conservative chancellor, George Osborne (Ganesh 2014: 173). The updated edition took stock of New Labour's 13 years in office, but it also contained frank reflections on what would become some of New Labour's political legacy: a fizzled-out modernization within David Cameron's Conservative Party and a vociferous ambiguity within the Labour Party about New Labour's legacy. On the latter, Gould wrote (2011: 399): "At no point will the dust quietly settle over New Labour." He was right, the dust has not settled, and it certainly has not been quiet. That is the topic of this book.

Over a decade and half has passed since Tony Blair ceased to be prime minister, yet throughout those years New Labour has been a bone of contention. My central argument is that different interpretations of New Labour – held by different people in the Labour Party – can explain much of the change in the party's direction since 2010. What came afterwards for Labour during the Miliband and Corbyn years was often thought up and framed in contradistinction, politically, to the Blair and Brown years. We can see this in relation to ideology, in the party's role in our democracy and in Labour's political style. In making this argument, I explore how the Labour Party made sense of New Labour after Gordon Brown left office in 2010, and how this process of defining New Labour's legacy affected the party's trajectory in opposition. Gould offered a preliminary analysis of why the New Labour years would prove to be controversial and a topic of debate in deciding the party's future. "There will be endless revision and rein-terpretation – about Iraq, about delivery and change and how much was or was not achieved, about Labour's economic record, equality, immigration, and the nature and success of public sector reform", Gould wrote (*ibid.*: 400):

> For a government criticized so often for its timidity and lack of bold-ness, the legacy of New Labour could hardly be more discordant. It has not, like so many other governments, slipped quietly into the long night; everyone has a view, angry and heartfelt. Some are passionately supportive, believing that New Labour is the only way to succeed; oth-ers believe just as passionately that we stood for nothing and achieved little. Few are neutral about New Labour.

There are important things to take from this, telling us much about the repercussions *for* Labour *of* New Labour. The effects of the wars in Iraq and Afghanistan have been wide ranging and often deeply tragic and traumatiz-ing: for Iraqis and Afghans, and for those in the military and their families. For Britain, the Iraq War in particular has an ongoing domestic legacy in terms of foreign policy. Blair's continuing belief in the rightness of his approach – in re-lation to both Iraq and Afghanistan – has contributed to a continued divide in British politics, particularly within Labour's politics. For Gordon Brown, the global financial crisis in 2007–8 ultimately came to define his time as prime min-ister. The political choices that followed, particularly the Conservative Party's adoption of austerity and the narration of a banking crisis as Labour's debt crisis, were attached to Labour's political identity for the next decade. Brown's actions to recapitalize Britain's banks, and to push for global cooperation to prevent a long-lasting depression, are juxtaposed in Labour's politics with the end of Labour's ambitions for public spending, "light-touch" regulation of the financial sector, trust in the economic benefits of globalization and an acceptance of the need for "tough decisions". As such, the economic pain felt by many people, the vast majority of whom were a world away from the continued wealth of banking, was connected to New Labour's legacy.

On top of "events" are the people involved and the judgements they made, something else Gould noted (*ibid.*). Blair and Brown dominated British poli-tics for over a decade. Labour leaving office coincided with their combined absence from the day-to-day life of the party. As with the stage set for James Graham's play, *Labour of Love*, the leader's photo on constituency office walls changed, and a new(ish) political cast stood in front of the voters. "Big" figures so often rarely want to "hang around", like ghosts haunting their successors. Yet the leading figures of New Labour never really left front-line politics, and their evolving legacies were and are felt by their successors. The generation of Labour politicians that followed Blair and Brown – many of whom worked for them as close advisors for more than a decade – meant the fuzzy factions associated with them (Blairites and Brownites) lived on, albeit without Blair and Brown providing day-to-day meaning for what became empty labels. And the institutions of British politics (including the media) were very keen to report on their memoirs or receive their analysis of Labour's post-2010 choices (something that continues today). For some observers of the party, Labour's move into opposition should have coincided with political retirement for New Labour's principals (Toynbee 2010). For others, that Blair had been in power for a decade, with Brown alongside and then succeeding him as Labour prime minister, meant that of course these "big beasts" needed to be heard.

Who's afraid of the big, bad Tony?

This takes us to Tony Blair himself – the leading member of the New Labour generation. New Labour and Blair are one and the same for many people – and therefore views of Blair the man impact upon views of the entire period of New Labour in office. A look at what Labour Party members think of Blair and Brown tells us a lot about the strength of feeling. In a 2021 poll, 83 per cent of Labour members who were asked had a "very" or "somewhat" favourable view of Gordon Brown. For Tony Blair, that dropped to 55 per cent (YouGov 2021). The two were side by side in opposition and in power yet have divergent political reputations within the Labour Party. In terms of political impact on British politics and, arguably, their respective parties, Blair is sometimes compared to Margaret Thatcher. Yet on this point (party popularity) there is a big difference: Thatcher remains overwhelmingly popular with Conservative members. Indeed, 93 per cent had a favourable view in one poll (YouGov 2019). Thatcher did not leave office at a time of her choosing, and neither did Blair (although he had accepted he would soon leave). Both had an ongoing and, at times, negative immediate impact on their political parties: for example, Thatcher encouraged Eurosceptic sentiment at a time of rebellion, and the Labour Party used a general menace of "Thatcherism" to characterize Conservative spending cuts in the early 2000s.

For the Conservative Party, however, the question of Thatcher as a good or bad political figure has been addressed, and there is close to a consensus among Conservative members. I am not suggesting there is no ideological disagreement within British Conservatism, nor that Thatcherism and Thatcher's legacy are not fought over, or irrelevant, far from it. But on the *status* of a leader and how much day-to-day political infighting is related to her tenure, the situation with Blair is simply incomparable. Why? It might be, as some have argued, that Blair seemed to take on some of Labour's traditions (Davis & Rentoul 2019: 300), although Thatcher took on some of her party's traditions too. What seems more likely is that the distance between Blair and his party seemed to increase with every year of office and continued after Blair departed Number 10 (Hindmoor & Pike 2022: 264). If you asked a Conservative Party member today whether Thatcher was a Conservative, I suspect you would receive a resounding "yes". If you asked a Labour Party member whether Blair was a socialist, or a social democrat, you may receive a resounding "no", a resounding "yes", or perhaps more often a mumble and the use of the word "progressive". For Blair and Labour, it is more complicated than with Thatcher and the Conservatives.

There are many other factors to consider about these ongoing effects. New Labour won three successive general elections, something no other Labour Party "project" has achieved. The party wanted to return to winning ways after defeat in 2010, and understandably looked to the near past for guidance about what to do and what not to do. A lot of Labour's policy record was uncontroversial, leaving some supporters (including many of the party's MPs) wondering why their fellow members seemed uncomfortable with what New Labour had done with its time in power. The ingredients for an immediate "row" were there. Don't abandon a winning formula, some said. Look at how many millions deserted Labour, others countered. Be proud of the minimum wage and new schools, some proffered. Beware private finance initiatives (PFIs) and New Labour's failure to tackle economic inequality, others argued. And of course, as David Cameron and George Osborne continued to press what they saw as the winning electoral message of Labour's alleged profligacy, successive leaders and shadow cabinet members found themselves talking about the previous Labour government, whether they wanted to or not.

Fast forward a decade and where are we? Labour is onto its third elected leader since Brown. Ed Miliband won the 2010 leadership election as, he noted, the "'moving on from New Labour' candidate" (Campbell 2018a). Indeed, other accounts have suggested that Miliband told friends, privately "that he wanted to bury New Labour" (Cowley & Kavanagh 2016: 70). By the time Jeremy Corbyn was the front-runner for the Labour leadership in 2015, Blair himself intervened. In an article with the headline, "Tony Blair: Even if you hate me, please don't take Labour over the cliff edge", Blair wrote (2015): "It doesn't matter whether you're on the left, right or centre of the party, whether you used to support me or hate me. But please understand the danger we are in." Corbyn duly won, and after a tumultuous two years surprised almost everyone by depriving Conservative Prime Minister Theresa May of a majority in the 2017 general election. Labour lost, but it had not been annihilated, as Blair had warned. There were many things to take from the result, but one thing – in the eyes of one Corbyn-friendly commentator – was super-clear: New Labour, or "Blairism", was "dead" (Jones 2017). The passing of another two and a bit very eventful years saw Labour lose the 2019 election to a resurgent, hard Brexit-supporting Conservative Party. Keir Starmer was elected as Labour's new leader. Yet in some ways the conversation remained similar. Following an interview with the *Financial Times*, and the headline "Starmer urges Labour to embrace Blair's legacy as he vows to win next election" (Parker 2021), the party was back in familiar territory – with New Labour as a "touchstone": an orientation point for visions of what the party should or should not be.

The list of why New Labour is the topic of so much debate is long. There are objective facts that cannot be denied: that New Labour legislated for particular things, or that it won majorities in three elections and failed to win one in 2010. But in this book, I am most interested in the subjective and the intersubjective: in other words, the beliefs people hold about something (in this case, New Labour) and some of the shared beliefs that people hold. This takes us to studying and analysing meanings. What has New Labour meant to people, and how have those meanings affected Labour's trajectory since 2010? Part of the job of studying politics is to provide some structure for understanding these things – frameworks for analysing the multitude of meanings that constitute our social world, politics being a big part of that world. There are many frameworks from which to choose from: for example, studies of politics that look at who was and was not voting for a political party and why; historical analyses, sometimes referred to as "thick description" in political science, that provide an account of what happened in the past, identifying certain causes. The framework I use here is an "interpretive" one; that is, an approach focused on the beliefs people in and around the Labour Party hold, the interpretations they come to and the resultant judgements that they make. Such approaches focus in particular on shared beliefs – what I referred to above as intersubjective beliefs – and how these shape our understanding of the world (Bevir & Blakely 2018). While the term "interpretive" is associated with a late twentieth-century move in the social sciences, many political scientists and philosophers have shown how important it is to understand the role of interpretation in how we think and in what we do. New Labour is subject to many different shared beliefs in and around the Labour Party, and it is those shared beliefs that matter most in the argument presented here.

Michael Freeden, a political theorist and expert on ideologies, demonstrated how an ideology could be understood as "combinations of political concepts organized in a particular way" (1996: 75). These concepts – things such as freedom or equality – relate to one another in different ways within different ideologies, thus providing a distinctive view of society and how to change it. Aside from core concepts, there are also "narratives, myths, symbols, idioms, or the affectivity of language" (*ibid.*: 5) that help us understand ideologies and how they matter to people. On this point, Henry Drucker, a political scientist who wrote the classic book *Doctrine and Ethos in the Labour Party*, added a rich interpretation of the Labour Party. He divided Labour's ideology into two parts: a doctrine and an ethos. The distinction is an important one, and it is similar to the articulation by Freeden. "Ethos", according to Drucker, included "the traditions, beliefs, characteristic procedures and feelings which help to animate the members of the party" (1979: 1). Strong feelings about New Labour have been catalysing debate and changes of direction within Labour for over a decade. Importantly, this is not a simple matter of cause and effect but of interpretation and political ideas. As the philosopher Mary Midgley wrote (2011: 3): "The way in which we imagine the world determines what we think important in it." There is plenty of imagination, and interpretation, on display from Labour's political actors in what follows.

Debates within Labour's "broad church"

Not everybody within the Labour Party begins at the same starting point, nor follows the same route through their time as a party member; or, indeed, as an interested observer of the party, chronicler of Labour or political columnist influencing the views of politicians and members alike. I discuss these different actors as "people in and around the Labour Party" in this book, influenced by other work looking at change within political parties and the range of people involved (e.g., Bale 2023). There are competing traditions within political parties, and as political fortunes rise and fall, and members join and leave, different traditions rise and fall too (Pike 2021). Drucker noted that "the ideology of the British Labour Party is, like the party itself, a tumultuous alliance of diverse parts. To ask, as a few always will, what is the 'real socialism' in the ideology is to ask the wrong question; it is also to demonstrate an intolerant temperament, a temperament out of harmony with the ethos of the party" (1979: 68). Clement Attlee, Labour's postwar prime minister (1945–51) and now a thoroughly defactionalized figure (popular with all), wrote much the same some 40 years prior. "I have seen a good many leaders of revolt arise, and very often, to use an expressive phrase, I have seen them meet themselves coming back", he wrote (1937: 8). Owing to "the heterogeneity of the sources from which the movement drew its inspiration", Attlee argued, it follows that "the Labour Party has always comprised people of very various outlooks, and that its note has always been one of comprehensiveness" (*ibid.*: 30).

This, in essence, describes both the origins and maintenance of Labour's "broad church": a famous phrase within the party connected with political pluralism, and an environment conducive to those "very various outlooks". In this book, I group some of the debates and themes within Labour's broad church

– influenced by Drucker and other work on Labour's identity – into three areas: ideology, democracy and politics. There will be points that are not captured by these three themes, and they relate to one another too, which is something I consider in the chapters that follow. But as a representation of the variety of Labour identities within the party's broad church, they help us understand differences of view. And, significantly, they help us comprehend important ways in which New Labour has been interpreted and how and why its legacy has been divisive. Drucker's *Doctrine and Ethos in the Labour Party* was similarly wide ranging in its consideration of the party, in the sense that the book covered ideology and concepts (e.g. equality) and some detailed policy discussion (in Drucker's case, "planning"), as well as Labour's relationship with its past, the role of the labour movement and the party's internal democracy colliding with the British political system, to name a few (Drucker 1979). There are undoubtedly great strengths to works of analysis that, in contrast to Drucker, focus on one particular aspect of a political party, for instance its economic policies or how it selects candidates. But there are great strengths, too, in providing a broader view, seeking to provide insights into how we can understand a political party and its politics. The framework of this book attempts to do just that.

The topic of ideology includes a great deal, but I focus on longstanding debates throughout Labour's history over the articulation of a clear "vision", something that has appeared in much critical commentary on Keir Starmer's leadership. The argument in favour of thinking through an ideology is a simple one: if you want to change things in practice, you need a theory to guide you. The argument against such thinking presents the "theoretical" and the "practical" as a dichotomy, with the former considered abstract, indulgent and often irrelevant to voters. I am convinced that the practical and the theoretical necessarily go together, as Mary Midgley persuasively argued (2000: 19):

> Perhaps … Realism and Idealism are *not* alternatives but two inseparable aspects of any true practical attitude. Our tendency to divide them is, however, remarkably strong. It is shown, rather comically, when people say (as they so often do) that some proposal is "all right in theory but no good in practice". A proposal that really *is* no good in practice has surely got something wrong with it in theory too.

This topic is always a prescient one for a party committed to social and political change to achieve social justice. The present time is a case in point: financial crises, and most recently the pandemic, have impacted the entire globe, and in the UK have shone a light on longstanding inequalities within our society. Unless you get to grips with exactly how and why this is the case, what hope do you have of changing it? This debate often gets going when the party is kicked out of office. Shirley Williams, who left the Labour Party and helped form the Social Democratic Party in 1981, wrote at the time of how "the intellectual winds now blow from a different quarter; the right-wing thinkers show more energy and confidence than do left-wing thinkers, many of whom reiterate tired and irrelevant dogmas or seem incapable of moving beyond their last stated position" (1981: 28). Labour had left office in 1979 and wouldn't return to power until 1997. It was losing ideologically and electorally. Writing over the second half of the twentieth century, Ralph Miliband – David and Ed's father – argued along similar lines, albeit from a different ideological perspective, suggesting that an "adherent" of "labourism", a term used to describe Labour's particular outlook, "frequently made a virtue of their 'practical' sense, their rejection of 'theory'" (2015: 291).

Democracy encompasses how Labour functions as a political movement and what democratic aspirations it has; from what its members do, to the role of a political party in enhancing democratic participation and empowering citizens. "Democracy", the Canadian philosopher Charles Taylor wrote (2022: 47), "is not what a majority at this moment or that happens to want. It is a project of greater empowerment and inclusion, liberty, equality, and solidarity for the future." For Taylor, "democracy" has more than one meaning. There is an "electoral criterion", which can be broadly understood as "on/off": you either have universal suffrage, and "free and fair" elections, or you don't (*ibid.*: 19). And there is a connected but much broader meaning, where everyone feels empowered within a democracy to affect what happens (*ibid.*: 20). It is this second part that led Taylor to describe democracy as a "telic concept"(*ibid.*: 19), in that it involves aiming for certain values or goals that may never be completely realized (Calhoun 2022: 48). Democracy is not purely a historically contingent thing, a product of a certain time, although that clearly matters too. It is also "defined by standards that can never be met" (Taylor 2022: 19). Those standards are the familiar, progressive values quoted from Taylor above. The separating out of these meanings of democracy does not mean – and Taylor did not suggest this – that the "electoral" part is simple and easy to maintain. Around the world, including in the UK, democratic institutions and practices have been attacked. To achieve a democracy which is truly "on" is a constant struggle.

In this book, though, my focus is on the telic meaning of democracy: the efforts towards empowerment and solidarity that never stop. Taylor's thinking is useful for understanding democracy and the Labour Party, not only in the past but right now, as politicians act within a context characterized as one of crisis and "democratic recession" (Wolf 2023: 81). In terms of history, Labour was not founded by politicians acting through a political ideology. It sprang from the trade union movement, organizing with socialists and others who were politically engaged. In other words, from the grassroots to high politics. As such, the values Taylor addressed – how to empower, build solidarity through social movements and challenge inequality – are all relevant to what Labour has always been. Understood as a set of traditions that are over a century old, Labour does not aspire merely to a "high politics" approach to democracy as it is currently constituted but to the telic concept of democracy. In terms of today, these traditions and ideas have found a new lease of life in pressing circumstances: specifically the attack upon "liberal democracy" from reactionary and populist politics. Ed Miliband has argued (2021a) that "representative" democracy – broadly understood as the election of people into positions of responsibility to undertake duties on our behalf – is essential but insufficient for today. "I don't think representative democracy is enough on its own in the era we're living in", he said, "partly because the problems are too complex, partly because people – and this is a good thing – have higher expectations of their involvement, and so we should be experimenting ... we should have a great wave of democratic experimentation ... it's got to be about people wielding power".

Through this argument, in addition to representative democracy, more participatory models of democracy (Sartori 1987: 113–16) are required. Trade unionism has long been a part of this, yet the power of the trade unions has been weakened by changes since the 1980s, including through legislative changes by Conservative governments. The challenges for how to increase the number of and empower democratic citizens are different today, but joining a (smaller) trade union movement are the social movements confronting the challenges of our time: racism, climate change, misogyny and threats to the right to protest. Labour's posture towards these movements, as well as more localized community groups, is key to its objective of democratic empowerment.

Politics, finally, speaks to the way Labour conducts itself and how people in and around the party make political choices. When Jeremy Corbyn told Labour's annual conference in 2016 that "our party is about campaigning and it's about protest too" as well as governing (Corbyn, 2016), he was speaking about this very broad topic. As was Tony Blair when he argued – in the same year – that there were "two types of politicians on the left, and there always have been". There was Blair, "whose face is on the placard" as an object of protest, and there was Corbyn, "the guy with the placard". The familiar distinction Blair made was between "the politics of power ... [and] the politics of protest" (Waugh 2016). This distinction is, for Blair, a dichotomy. For others who have studied the different motivations for political action, there are different political styles, although the Blair dichotomy may often be a false one. Frank Parkin, a sociologist who researched the Campaign for Nuclear Disarmament in the 1960s, argued that rarely was any one person on the left fully "instrumental" (motivated by the politics of power) or fully "expressive" (motivated by expressing one's beliefs), although "a greater orientation towards one of the two styles is normally discernible" (Parkin 1968: 34). Such a categorization is useful, and indeed Blair himself has previously demonstrated a more "expressive" political approach (see Pike & Hindmoor 2020; Pike 2019).

In this book, however, I move beyond this approach of categorizing political styles. Instead, I aim to get to the roots of such characterizations, which I argue are the different beliefs and emotions that inform day-to-day moral judgements in politics. Here, the philosophical inspiration is Bernard Williams and his thinking about moral "sensibility" in politics (1981: 63). Take the examples from Corbyn and Blair above. When Corbyn talked of "protest", he was referring to an idea of politics that includes a role for opposing what a political actor – regardless of whether they are a politician or not – sees as wrong, and in conflict with their values. To not stand up and oppose something that does conflict with a person's values would be wrong. When Blair contrasted the politics of "power" with that of "protest", he revealed a different judgement. Politics, so goes this argument, necessarily involves "tough decisions" – something Williams recognized too – and as such, politicians must prove themselves capable of taking the "tough" choice if they really want to gain power. This way of thinking, as I explore later, formed an important part of New Labour's legacy, and was something that some people in and around the Labour Party reacted against strongly. The essential insight from Williams, which I discuss in detail in this book, is that different moral outlooks – specifically around recognizing the "moral cost" of political decision-making (Williams 1981: 63) – help explain these different political approaches.

Structure of the book

Chapters 1–3 take the above themes – ideology, democracy and politics – as topics for analysing how New Labour's legacy has affected the party's trajectory since 2010. Breaking it down in this way, we see how different interpretations of New Labour led to course corrections and different objectives for the Labour Party after Blair and Brown. From this, we can also understand why New Labour's legacy has been so contentious, and saw the party move away from New Labour across all three areas. People in and around the Labour Party presented much post-2010 politics as being in contradistinction to how New Labour had come to be perceived: that New Labour had overseen the party losing its socialist or social democratic underpinning, had shrivelled the party as a democratic movement and had ceased to weigh the moral costs of its focus on power. The book then turns to the future: Keir Starmer's leadership and Labour's future. Chapter 4 presents my case for what the party should do next, based on the three themes of the book and in the context of a changing UK politics since

2019, including a strengthening of Labour's Westminster opinion poll ratings, a cautious optimism for Scottish Labour under Anas Sarwar's leadership and amid dramatic and negative headlines for the Scottish National Party (SNP), and a reforming Welsh Labour government working on innovative policies such as piloting a basic income for care leavers turning 18. Chapter 4 – a political essay – makes the case for a more ideologically confident Labour Party with a distinctive political economy that could stand the test of time. In the Conclusion, I return to the core argument of the book and try to answer the obvious question: has the current Labour Party gotten over New Labour?

Chapter 1 looks at ideology, from when Brown left Downing Street to where Labour finds itself today. The 2010 leadership contest became a story of the Miliband brothers and (fairly or unfairly) two different inheritances from New Labour: a continuation of a "Blairite" direction, applied to David Miliband, and a more critical, although not entirely "Brownite" direction, applied to Ed Miliband. This chapter offers two key arguments for understanding Labour's ideology after New Labour, pointing to some (perhaps surprising) similarities between the Miliband and Corbyn leaderships. The chapter shows how both the Miliband brothers and key figures during the Corbyn years – such as John McDonnell – believed in the need for Labour to turn to ideas after New Labour. These key figures believed in the power of ideas to renew Labour's project and were critical of New Labour's gradual shift away from any coherent, left ideology. I then explain *how* these key actors believed Labour's ideology needed to change. On this, there is a consistency from Ed Miliband to Jeremy Corbyn, and a difference, both reinforced by the need to "get over" New Labour.

The Miliband and Corbyn leaderships can be located within what the sociologist Mike Savage has termed the "inequality paradigm" (2021: 2), a shift in how we interpret and understand the social world, and one which "fundamentally unsettles long-term assumptions about the direction and nature of social change" (*ibid.*). Savage's argument brought together a number of different paradigmatic features: the importance of new approaches to social science, visualizations of inequality, how what he termed the "weight of the past" had become more "salient" (*ibid.*: 94) in the years since the global financial crisis and – following on from that – how the inequality paradigm has continued to develop, with social movements throughout the world taking a stand against racism, misogyny and sexual violence (*ibid.*: 197–8). Inspired by Savage's argument, I focus specifically on a post-financial crisis ideational turn in politics and society. As Stanley noted, "notions of 'the 1 per cent' and the 'rigged system' have become core features of British politics" (2022: 106). This "turn" within British politics helps us comprehend the shared ideological framing Miliband and Corbyn embraced to "get over" New Labour, yet there was a key difference.

For reasons I explore in Chapter 1, Miliband did not overcome a strategic hesitancy to – borrowing a term from his 2021 book – "go big" (Miliband 2021b). Corbyn's project easily shook off this hesitancy – although this was not without its flaws – and sought to draw a contrast with a "managerialist" approach associated with New Labour. The biggest obstacle to Corbynism as a unified ideological project was Brexit. Corbynism remained a bold project but lost the battle between a "1 per cent and 99 per cent" strategy and the dominant "52 per cent versus 48 per cent" of a Brexit election. Today, Keir Starmer has overseen something of a counter-reaction to the Miliband and Corbyn years, but if "Starmerism" is associated within anything above all else, it is with a leader still making up his mind. Starmer won the Labour leadership by continuing the message of his predecessors, yet he swiftly began searching for something else. The contemporary Labour Party has retained some distinctive progressive policies, and the Labour leader has found a narrative – around "missions" thinking – that he is more comfortable embodying. Yet Starmer's thinking, while including the admirable goal of reforming the state, is very technocratic. The absence of an ideological guide, in contrast to the previous decade, is now being felt by Labour.

Chapter 2 looks at how people in and around the Labour Party sought to experiment with different approaches to democracy, hoping to empower people and "become a movement again" after New Labour's focus on "command and control". More participatory approaches to democracy – trying to reach the goals that make democracy a telic concept in Taylor's phrase – are sometimes contrasted with the metaphor of "machine politics". This evocative metaphor says that instead of empowering people to act and have more control over their political, economic and social world, political parties treat those wanting to engage as cogs in a machine, harvesting votes for politicians jealously guarding their power. New Labour was widely perceived as having become that "machine". In Ed Miliband's words, there had been a "hollowing out of the movement and the party" during the New Labour years (2010b: 61). After 2010, Ed Miliband embraced – for a short time – a more "relational" approach to political campaigning (Ferguson 2013). However, while he was interested in the model of "community organizing" – where priorities come from grassroots campaigns and politics is co-produced – Miliband soon focused on other things after 2010.

As the Corbyn era commenced, Labour's membership increased hugely. Having been relatively stable at around 200,000 after 2010, the membership exceeded half a million during the Corbyn years (Burton & Tunnicliffe 2022: 11). Hundreds of thousands of people had responded to Corbyn's candidacy and leadership by joining the Labour Party, and many of them believed politics was, if not broken, in need of change (Whiteley *et al.* 2019: 95). The organization that sought to embody Corbyn's brand of campaigning optimism was Momentum, a group with aspirations to become a social movement. All of this was presented as the right response to New Labour's micro-management and "control freak-ery" (Minkin 2014: 5). "That top-down behaviour has to end", Corbyn claimed, "we make the best policy through inclusive democratic discussion" (2015b: 15). Yet things were not always that simple. Brexit demonstrated that "control freak-ery" was alive and well within Corbyn's Labour. Organizational culture is also hugely important for social movements, and on this, Corbyn's leadership failed – most importantly in tackling antisemitism within the Labour Party. Today, Starmer's Labour Party has been accused of strict party management – for ex-ample over selections for Labour Party parliamentary candidates (Elgot 2022c) – and the leadership has shown limited interest in thinking about "movement politics". Yet Labour's policy programme includes an ambitious approach to decentralizing political power. Changing the Labour Party, and adopting more participatory democratic ideas, will be necessary, I argue, if Labour succeeds in returning to government and shifting power away from the centre, as Starmer says he wants to.

Chapter 3 picks up on Labour's approach to politics after New Labour. As noted above, the everyday dichotomies that people in and around the Labour Party use when considering their approach to politics – "power versus protest", "head versus heart", "principle versus pragmatism" – tell us something, but they are not sufficient to comprehend why these debates exist in the first place. To answer this, Chapter 3 engages with Bernard Williams' moral philosophy and how we – as people – understand moral dilemmas and reach moral judgements. From Williams, I adopt an understanding of the "moral cost" involved in taking some political decisions. Williams considered such costs to be intrinsic to politi-cal life, with decisions, behaviours and practices in politics that are "morally dis-agreeable" (1981: 60). One of the questions Williams considered was the extent to which political actors acknowledge this. Williams identified a way of moral thinking which did not: utilitarianism (1981: 58–9). On the basis of Williams' critique of utilitarianism, I argue that where a political actor accepts this way of thinking, if there is a moral cost – particularly at the leadership level of a political party – it is through failing to win office and being powerless, and thereby not being able to deliver what is obviously (in the view of the actor) a greater good for a greater number of people. As such, the "moral costs" of day-to-day political judgements go unacknowledged in the shadow of this overarching claim.

Insufficient acknowledgement of moral cost – what came to be seen as the dominance of a utilitarian moral stance – formed a part of New Labour's legacy. My case in Chapter 3 is that Labour's political actors were much more alive to this dynamic after 2010, acknowledging the moral costs of accommo-dating Conservative arguments but still – inevitably – struggling with these judgements. Ed Miliband argued that New Labour had been wrong to tell the party that its politicians had to choose between "head" and "heart" (2010b: 63).

Pride in expressing Labour's "true" values was integral to Corbyn's campaign too. "Straight taking" politics would replace the spin still lingering after the New Labour years. Labour would be proud of its identity again, including its advocacy of the working class. Yet if New Labour had been all head and little heart, where was Corbyn's Labour when it came to opposing Brexit? Starmer's tenure has been notable for the leader's self-proclaimed ruthlessness in prioritizing a Labour election victory. As with the ideological journey from 2010 to today, on politics Starmer has led a counter-reaction to the post-2010 years, and who can argue with a leader wanting to win a general election? But having not made up his mind regarding what Labour is for, the focus on winning becomes a truism and risks being tautological: the rationale for winning is to win. Even a sympathetic view of the Starmer leadership would, I think, concur that the Labour leader has embraced what I call the "utilitarian presumption".

The book is not written as a straightforward, chronological narrative. While all three of the thematic chapters broadly follow a chronological approach, beginning with Ed Miliband's leadership and culminating with Keir Starmer's, they are focused on the specific topic considered in each chapter. Chapter 4 is focused on the contemporary Labour Party and makes a political case for the future. This means that some events – and some political intrigue – are absent from the book or more directly relevant to one of the themes, and so they are missing from the other chapters. The main reason for this approach is because what makes this book different to the (excellent) narrative accounts that have emerged is the way of looking at Labour's politics that I try to convey. The story I am trying to tell is a distinctive one: how interpretations of New Labour have affected the party's trajectory since 2010. I try to tell that story through different academic lenses, derived not only from traditions of Labour Party scholarship but from work in political theory and philosophy that is rarely applied to the study of British politics and political parties. One of the features of political science should be to bring together concepts that help us understand politics, and to develop those concepts through application to "actually existing" politics. I hope this book does that. Such an approach is somewhat "realist" (Geuss 2008: 9–11), and it takes seriously both outcomes and the significance of context (*ibid.*: 11–15).

All three chapters have something in common: the themes – ideology, democracy and politics – and how they have developed over this early part of the twenty-first century are pressing matters in our political and social world. They are not distinctive to the Labour Party. The "inequality paradigm", of course, is not about the Labour Party; it is much bigger than that. So too the "crisis" of democracy that so many have written about and the efforts at building a more participatory and equal political system in response to reactionary politics across the world. Similarly, when thinking about the way we conduct politics, we have experienced a great deal of upheaval in the first two and a bit decades of the twenty-first century: what some have labelled an "age of anger" (Mishra 2016), including politicians who have plunged political discourse and practice to greater depths of depravity and vulgarity. Out of all of this has emerged political innovation too: progressive responses to the risks and dreadfulness that contemporary politics contains. US politician Alexandria Ocasio-Cortez is a good example of a left political actor who has rooted her politics in tackling inequality and facing up to the climate emergency, fostered a more participatory and community-based democracy, and included a role for protesting the morally objectionable alongside the evidence-based, legislative scrutiny that democratic politics involves. In short, while this book is about Labour, it is also a book about our times and how some people on the left of politics have responded. The debates and arguments about the themes, therefore, have a wider relevance. Indeed, they should also be seen – certainly in terms of their explanatory power – as examples of an interpretive reaction to perceived wrong turns and past mistakes within social democracy more broadly, as diagnosed by academics (see, e.g., Berman & Snegovaya 2019) as well as activists and politicians.

The legacies of New Labour

As noted above, across all three areas of analysis the book shows how, after 2010, the Labour Party attempted to move away from how New Labour came to be perceived. Different actors succeeded in this move to different extents and at times failed their own tests for "getting over" New Labour. These strategic moves were taken on the basis of beliefs and judgements about the political context and the beliefs of others (Hay 2002: 126–34). Actors made these moves in the context of party traditions of varying strengths. In terms of interpretations of New Labour, there is no one "legacy" agreed upon by Labour's political actors; rather there is an assortment of perceived legacies, impacting Labour's contemporary politics at different times and in different ways. From the perspective I offer in this book, I have perhaps added another: that a legacy of New Labour has been the stimulation of much political change within the party, reached in contradistinction to the politics New Labour came to represent. There are numerous "drivers" of party change (Bale 2012: 316–17). The interpretive approach I adopt here brings a number of these together, understood through the different interpretations of New Labour held by various actors. Since Keir Starmer has begun to establish a leadership identity, there has been something of a counter-reaction to the views of his predecessors, with New Labour subject to some reputational rehabilitation. It is much too simplistic, however, to view Starmer's Labour as a "tribute act". More precisely, a re-evaluation is underway: a questioning of the moving away from New Labour and a renewed fondness for some of New Labour's famous rhetoric. I address this point in more detail in Chapter 4.

It is worth noting here that, as with those "in and around the Labour Party" – who are my focus in this book – academics and political analysts more generally have also engaged in the battle over New Labour. We have seen interventions that sought to bring "balance" to the debate or to celebrate/condemn a political project for its perceived distance – or lack of – from New Labour. It is worth journeying back for a moment to consider how academic interpretations of New Labour began, and noting a commonality with today: a fascination with New Labour, apparent at the very outset of the project, and heightened first by the inevitability of a Blair victory, then by New Labour's actual electoral triumph. In the late 1990s, Blair's rhetoric and political style appeared to project the confidence of a prosperous nation, and the Conservative Party was feeling sorry for itself. The urgency of understanding New Labour – this political phenomenon – was partnered with a curiosity about how to categorize New Labour in relation to existing models of social democracy (see Driver & Martell 2006). Alongside this came a scepticism about Blair's success. Thatcherism had been the dominant, hegemonic political project of the 1980s, and the Labour Party – from Neil Kinnock becoming leader onwards – had dropped some key left-wing policies, including unilateral nuclear disarmament and ambitions for nationalization, while remaining rhetorically (and, I would argue, substantively) opposed to Thatcherism.

Blair, following his predecessors, embraced the need to accommodate Labour to Thatcherite politics (Heffernan 2000: 27). Labour's "modernization" had been a "metaphor for the politics of 'catch-up' ... one informed not by post-war social democracy, but by Labour's accommodation to and adaption of Thatcherism's neo-liberal political agenda" (*ibid.*: 178). Accounts of this nature owed much to a "rational choice" understanding of politics: that to compete, politicians would often accommodate to shifting political ground, and following Thatcherism that move was a neoliberal one. Murphy has made the important point that timing is very relevant here. Early criticisms of New Labour, depicting an accommodation with neoliberalism, "were still hampered by the fact that most of them appeared in the late 1990s and early 2000s – in other words, before Labour's biggest increases in public services spending arrived" (Murphy 2023a: 232). I return to the importance of time – the passage of time and what a governing record looks like relative to what comes afterwards – in the Conclusion.

Some early analyses of New Labour did detect more political subtlety and qualify the more "rationalistic" accounts with greater complexity. Finlayson (2003: 9) sought to locate New Labour within an "underlying 'doxa'" – a kind of ideational context – and as such, while the project was a "symptom" of an assortment of things (*ibid.*: 41), the architects of New Labour also meant what they said (*ibid.*: 39–40). Something similar can be read from Colin Hay's influential work on New Labour. While the Labour Party *had* moved towards the Conservatives on the economy, this was a more complicated event than a rationalistic impulse to accommodate in the interests of party competition. The key actors at the top of New Labour bought into globalization (another aspect of New Labour's legacy that I return to throughout the book), something that was not unique to Britain, nor to Labour (Hay 1999: 136). The extent to which a political party can shape its environment is a classic debate within political science and has been at the centre of academic interpretations of New Labour (see also Hindmoor 2004).

This remains important not only for how academics study political parties but for how any interested observer interacts with the Labour Party. Labour politicians have choices, of course, but they also perceive constraints: political, economic, organizational and even technical or logistical. Judgement, then, surely becomes the focus. Is Labour pushing hard enough for social democratic or socialist objectives? Does the party even really believe in them, or are ambitious social democratic or socialist objectives always easily jettisoned, guilt-free, to achieve power? Jackson, writing during the Corbyn leadership and reflecting on two decades since New Labour's 1997 victory, rightly pointed to a connected debate: that of the "longevity of Labour governments" (2018: 4). Jackson's argument was that, in being cautious about what they could and could not do in their electoral and economic environment, Blair and Brown were attempting to extend the duration of Labour in power beyond one term. Such caution could, then, be rewarded: if the changes a party makes, over time, cannot be easily undone, the duration of power is an important part of a political strategy. This is something New Labour also misjudged, in part because, Jackson suggested, of an overconfidence that what New Labour represented – distributing the proceeds of (relatively strong) growth without too much meddling in the working of the economy – would become a lasting political consensus (*ibid.*). Following the financial crisis, of course, such a consensus – represented, as it had been, by Conservative concessions to Labour spending – ended.

With Labour out of power, scholars began their contributions to legacy construction. Diamond (2021) took on the "myths" of New Labour scholarship and commentary, including the idea that New Labour – as with Heffernan – had been an accommodation with Thatcherism, rather than, as Diamond countered, an "intellectual undertaking" of its own (2021: 4), emanating from political debates on the social democratic and socialist left. The historian Jon Davis, along with the experienced journalist (and biographer of Blair) John Rentoul, set about preparing a corrective to anti-Blair feeling, first through teaching, then publishing a book (2019) and finally providing historical advice for a BBC documentary about New Labour: one dismissed as "hagiography" by a critic (Steers 2021). The authors noted that Blair had found himself "disowned by many in his own party", with "Blairite" having become "an insult of choice" (Davis & Rentoul 2019: 1–2). Their focus was on "good government": the idea that with governments setting out to do things and encountering challenges along the way, a reasonable evaluation tool is whether they achieved anything they set out to do. On this point, Davis and Rentoul were positive about Blair and his achievements, writing in the hope "that time will eventually see Blair's reputation in some way repaired" (*ibid.*: 13).

Another interesting contribution came from Chris Clarke (2020), who wrote a defence of what he called "left pluralism" (within which was a more positive view of New Labour) against "left populism" (which was critical of New Labour). Interpretations of New Labour provided a kind of ideational background to Clarke's book: one of the many dividing lines between these two left positions (*ibid.*: 8). Enveloped by the characterization of populism, however, was sometimes anger at inequality or a belief that the Conservatives are very often completely wrong about things. The term "populism" has been saddled with too many meanings and been overused: in the words of one scholar, it can be subject to what is called "concept stretching" (van Kessel 2014: 115). It's possible to look at the politics of the last decade or more and regret that it has all been far from "rational". That "what matters is what works" – a famous New Labour refrain – appeared to be chucked out of a Whitehall window and taken by the wind, perhaps to Emmanuel Macron's France or as far away as Justin Trudeau's Canada. To the extent that very few people would want to embrace bad ideas, these regrets are valid. But opposition to some bad ideas does not add up to a coherent political ideology, and no substantive political outlook is devoid of emotion, tradition or powerful beliefs that affect both how people see the world and what decisions they make. Blair's critics, meanwhile, have continued to write about the party through the prism of perceived proximity to New Labour, with Corbyn's leadership seen as the culmination of years of resistance within the Labour Party (Panitch & Leys 2020: 28). Oliver Eagleton used the term "Newest Labour" to critique Starmer's leadership and his policy stances (2022: 172). Here, association with Blairite terms is simply bad.

In Chapter 4 and the Conclusion, I look to the future and attempt to move on, in my own way, by avoiding further litigation on the topic of New Labour. Chapter 4 sets out what I think Labour's overarching politics should look like in the coming decade. It is informed by the analysis presented in this book and draws upon the three themes of ideology, democracy and politics. I start the chapter by locating Keir Starmer's politics within the tradition of "labourism", in particular highlighting a tendency to avoid any articulation of a "good society". While I concede that labourism is an imperfect term, it still speaks to a kind of Labour politics that lacks both ideological confidence and ambition. Here

I make the claim that Labour is still too fearful of Conservatism. Through a critique of labourism, and a discussion of some political theory and philosophy (including G. A. Cohen and Axel Honneth), I make the case for a clearer set of ideological objectives, including clarity over "means" and "ends" and the prioritization of building institutions that foster different social relations: in short, a social democratic or socialist political economy.

The thinking I present on this speaks to the earlier discussion about Labour governments making a lasting difference. Ideological confidence is, I contend, integral to a future Labour government making meaningful change, governing beyond one electoral cycle and changing British politics – and British political economy – for the longer term. Writing about European social democracy in the 1980s, Esping-Andersen argued that "social democratic decomposition will result from a failure to institutionalize universalistic solidarity" (1985: 34), and that social democracy needed to "relieve the state of its sole responsibility" for solidarity to prevent "a backlash against the welfare state" (*ibid.*: 35). In other words, that we support one another needs to become part of a country's institutional fabric for social democracy to succeed, as does an understanding that the state should not be the only outlet for such an approach. This book charts some similar thinking. Yet sometimes Labour has overlooked or underthought the possibilities of its policies, particularly services it has funded or changes it has made to entitlements. Sure Start centres, for example, were not only childcare settings, they were locations for the building of citizen solidarity and the strengthening of local community groups and networks: state investment creating non-state solidarity. Winning the ideological contest for the continuation of such programmes is not, then, simply advocating for spending money (essential though that funding is). It is comprehending that investing in institutions can change how people communicate and act in communities over the longer term. When something like that is "cut" as a "cost", it is a cost to society.

I then move towards the more programmatic part of the chapter, making the case for ideas connected to three central objectives for Labour: rebuilding public services, facing up to the climate crisis and creating a more equal society. Labour has produced policies relevant to all three since 2019, yet – partly owing to its defensiveness and fear of Conservatism – it has ruled out many things that would make a big difference across all three objectives. On the green transition, Labour has generated big plans for investment, but it needs a stronger ideological orientation to see those plans through to their full potential. On public spending, I argue that Labour needs to get serious on tax. The British state needs more money, and for Labour to realize its core goals it needs to reform the tax system. And on Brexit, Labour must be prepared to debate with greater honesty and confront what may end up being the biggest political effort of a future Labour government: changing Britain's relations with the European Union (EU) towards much greater cooperation. Chapter 4 also touches on a number of other policy areas, from migration to the shift towards "modern supply-side economics". Overall, Chapter 4 is written in the tradition of the political essay: it makes the case for a clearer, more ambitious socialist or social democratic politics.

I conclude the book with some reflections on the following question: has the Labour Party gotten over New Labour? I break this question down into two broad parts: (1) the historical debate about the New Labour project and its governments and (2) people in and around the Labour Party thinking of New Labour as a "touchstone". On the historical debates – and on this I mean the debates people in and around the Labour Party have had – I suggest there is a modest reassessment underway, one that recognizes more complexity and nuance when it comes to New Labour. That is, I think, a good thing for the Labour Party. On the touchstone argument, the situation is less clear. It is possible that factionalism oriented around New Labour is much less present in the contemporary Labour Party, but its effect is still noticeable. I end the Conclusion with an argument that suggests we will still be talking about the relevance of New Labour in the years to come, not just as a historical debate but because of the current political conjuncture (in the UK and elsewhere) that seeks to move on from the politics of the 1990s, particularly the central role of globalization. We are in a "post-something" ideological age, by which I mean that what is being left behind is not yet fully clear. There is a move happening though, perhaps affected by the end of "post-politics" and the arrival of a different, more "political" time (Jäger 2023), although for some political actors that may still be an open question.

This book is not another critique or defence of the New Labour years, as should now be clear. Nor is it close to a history either of the New Labour years (of which there are a growing number, with more to come as New Labour-era government papers are gradually released) or the post-2010 years (a period that will no doubt be subject to its own detailed histories). Instead, this book explains how the political legacy of New Labour has affected – and continues to affect – the party's trajectory. Should a prime minister who left office approaching 20 years ago still be a touchstone for people in and around Labour, either for what to do or for what not to do? I think not. Some of this may come down to the ease with which Blair can be inserted into two longstanding, contrasting Labour Party narratives. To steer away from Blair is to fight against ideological surrender, which all but guarantees the party will betray its socialist instincts and not achieve much at all. To embrace Blair is to fight against the habit of losing, something that all but guarantees Labour will spend a great deal of time in the political wilderness. The New Labour years were the last time the party was in power, and therefore this period is directly relevant to these two powerful beliefs about betrayal and powerlessness. And many people involved in those years of office remain engaged with Labour's politics today, including acting as some of Keir Starmer's most senior advisors. If there is one thing Blair's central role in the two longstanding debates referred to above does show, it's that Tony Blair is very much a Labour Party person, whether people in and around the Labour Party like it or not.

1
IDEOLOGY: STUCK BETWEEN UTOPIA AND THE DOG AND DUCK

Introduction

"Bloody hell, not another Tony-Gordon scenario," Alastair Campbell said to David Miliband (Campbell 2018b: 567), "and even worse because you're brothers!" It was December 2009, and the New Labour years had reached their final months. Gordon Brown, then prime minister, was struggling with diminished political authority, having experienced cabinet resignations, dire poll ratings and relentless negative media. Thoughts were inevitably turning to what would happen next. While the Conservative leader, David Cameron, was not seen as running away with the forthcoming 2010 election, Labour MPs did not have high expectations for their party's performance. So, who would lead Labour after Brown? The name "Miliband" was typically the answer to that question, but increasingly people wondered, which one, David or Ed? David and Ed Miliband were both cabinet ministers in 2009, although with different political identities viewed through the prism of the leading figures of New Labour: Blair and Brown. What Campbell feared – having just heard from David Miliband that his brother was not convinced he should be the next Labour leader – was that the "TB-GBs" (the nickname given to the Blair–Brown feud in office) would be replicated with the Milibands (*ibid.*).

Ed and David did run against each other, along with Diane Abbott, Ed Balls and Andy Burnham, although it was very clearly, from day one, the "Miliband show". Ed Miliband beat his brother by a tiny margin, and the "psychodrama" label often attached to Blair and Brown was duly resurrected. The result was seen as a "surprise", yet five years later there was an even bigger one: the election of Jeremy Corbyn to succeed Miliband, who had been defeated in the 2015 election by Cameron's Conservatives, with the Tories winning a parliamentary majority against the odds. While the Miliband psychodrama became a distant memory, viewing Labour politics through the prism of New Labour did not. Blair himself became a more high-profile figure again, despairing at the Corbyn leadership and focusing on the Brexit debates that followed the 2016 referendum. The post-2010 years were tumultuous ones indeed. This chapter seeks to explain how successive Labour leaders sought to "get over" New Labour ideologically. There are two core arguments in what follows. The first is a point of similarity between the Miliband brothers and some of the leading lights of the Corbyn project, including John McDonnell, who would go on to be shadow chancellor after 2015. This is the belief that Labour – following New Labour – desperately needed ideological renewal. The party needed to take ideas seriously again. The Milibands had, and have, great faith in the power of ideas to affect politics. They believed that New Labour had become too distant from some of the party's ideational traditions and guiding concepts. This was key to Corbynism too. Post-2010 Labour pursued a return to ideas and the articulation of a revised ideology: a guide for the party to navigate the perennial storms and changing political landscape of British politics.

The second argument involves some key differences about *how* the party needed to "move on". Again, there is something that unites the Miliband and Corbyn leaderships: both were very clearly located within the collection of analyses and ideas present in what the sociologist Mike Savage has termed the "inequality paradigm" (2021: 2). In this chapter, I am particularly focused on the post-financial crisis ideational turn in politics *against economic inequality* (although, I should add, it was far from the only ideological development). This provided Ed Miliband and Jeremy Corbyn with an ideological frame to "get over" New Labour. Yet, for Miliband, this also presented significant political challenges: dilemmas that Corbyn would not struggle with but which hindered Miliband's mission. While committed to orienting Labour away from New Labour, Miliband was also part of a milieu which Corbyn was completely divorced from: a group of Labour politicians and advisors who governed during the New Labour years and were suspicious of "trashing the record". Miliband inhabited the worst of all worlds in some eyes: attacking New Labour on the failures exposed by the inequality paradigm while meekly defending New Labour on the public spending that had led to the rebuilding of public services and some egalitarian outcomes.

Corbyn and his allies were, of course, unhindered by these concerns. In the context of Miliband's electoral defeat, the above strategy – half-hearted compromise – could be judged an electoral and political failure. Yet "Milibandism" was not junked from an ideological point of view; what was ditched was the inhibition, along with a great deal of the reluctance to confront the challenges thrown up by the inequality paradigm with big, bold policies. Corbyn was very different from previous Labour leaders, of course, and I don't deny that in this book. Yet the "novelty" was not a return to a 1970s or 1980s socialist ideology. There are commonalities with the past because some solutions to inequality are enduring (and enduringly controversial in British politics). But Corbynism as an ideological project – which is the focus of this chapter – was located in the post-crash inequality paradigm, just as Milibandism was. The big difference was the ideological posture: it was no longer a political class afraid of the inevitable hostility to socialism that comes from some parts of the media. Of course, this was not without its flaws. Some came to see the lack of inhibition as leading to excessive self-confidence and hubris. Others, more sympathetically, pointed to a failure to prioritize or queried the politics of delivery (Meadway 2020).

Labour then entered "recovery" mode after four straight election defeats. The inequality paradigm has remained relevant to Keir Starmer's leadership, particularly as he confronted the everyday inequalities exposed by the pandemic, those raised by the campaigns of groups such as Black Lives Matter and long overdue debates about Britain's imperial past and systemic racism in British society. Yet Starmer's ideological flexibility has raised eyebrows. His commitments are readily made yet seemingly also readily dropped. Does this period mark the end of Labour's "ideas turn"? In short, I suggest the answer is "yes", although with the following caveat. Labour has maintained a programme containing some ambitious ideas. Starmer's politics is geared towards reform of the state and has a focus on delivery. He has been unapologetic about that. However, ideologically the story is of inconsistency and a lack of clarity. Starmer has not ignored all ideological debates, he has simply changed his mind a lot, appearing both more comfortable and consistent on matters considered to be "technocratic". The title of this chapter pits visions of utopia against the electoral reality of the Dog and Duck, a favoured journalistic shorthand for where "real" voters discuss the state of the nation (e.g., Robinson 2015: 176). Starmer – the very practical politician – has been seeking an election-winning message without (yet) making his mind up about what Labour is for.

"Brothers, not clones"

Shortly after becoming the MP for Doncaster North, Ed Miliband gave a speech at a conference marking 50 years since the publication of *The Future of Socialism*, one of the more famous works of socialist theorizing to come from the Labour Party, written by Anthony Crosland, MP for Great Grimsby and a cabinet minister before his untimely death in 1977. Crosland's "mark on the Labour Party and the intellectual life of the British Left is unusual", according to Diamond, for "the British labour movement was notoriously circumspect about intellectuals" (2016: 39). The enduring relevance of his contribution revealed "a vacuum contemporary politicians have struggled to fill" (*ibid.*: 44). The Miliband brothers both had ambitions to remedy this. In his speech in 2006, Ed Miliband made the case for the then Labour government to restate its mission. The context was Tony Blair's final year as prime minister, a moment when Blair's priorities appeared to be his own rather than Labour's (Hindmoor & Pike 2022: 256–7), and people queried what project would come next. Meanwhile, David Cameron – recently elected as Conservative leader – was pursuing his own "modernization" project. Cameron was seeking to shift Conservative positions on the environment and public services, something that acknowledged – according to Miliband – that the Conservatives had "lost the ideological battles of the last ten years" (Miliband 2006).

This made it important "that part of our renewal must be to restate our guiding mission – as Crosland taught. I am not suggesting that people ask on the doorstep – 'what's your guiding ideology?' But I think that is to miss the point. People do want to know what it is that motivates you ... Competence is necessary but not sufficient" (Miliband 2006).

Part of the significance of *The Future of Socialism* was, for Miliband, that it was "based on the notion that there is purpose in thinking through politics from a set of first principles, from an ideology" (*ibid.*). Having worked for Harriet Harman in Labour's pre-1997 opposition years, and then for Gordon Brown before entering government, Miliband was experienced and promoted quickly into ministerial office. Amid the transition from Blair to Brown – something that would see Ed Miliband promoted to the cabinet and charged with pulling together Labour's next manifesto – Miliband stuck to his message. He wrote, in a collection focused on a "new generation", that "what matters most to the course of political history is not simply the institutional legacy – institutions built by government – but the ideological legacy – the terrain in which politics is played out" (Miliband 2007: 39). "Renewal" in office, argued Miliband, necessitated a set of ideas that "can start at a high level of abstraction, but ... must be translatable into a framework for political action" (*ibid.*: 30). Miliband sketched out the themes that would be present in his leadership of the party a few years later: tackling inequality, along with what would become a key critique of New Labour, the "danger ... of a politics that becomes centred on managerialism and turns people off" (*ibid.*: 39). The foundations for both Ed Miliband's relatively critical take on New Labour and his alternative – an emphasis on equality – were built during the final years of New Labour. He conducted this intellectual exercise quietly, remaining a loyal member of Gordon Brown's cabinet, later becoming secretary of state for energy and climate change, and building a profile within the party.

David Miliband, meanwhile, was in a different position. Elected in 2001, and having served in a number of ministerial posts, Miliband was appointed foreign secretary by Gordon Brown in 2007 and as such was one of the most senior members of the government. Prior to Brown becoming Labour's leader and prime minister, there had been some talk from David Miliband's colleagues that he should consider running for the job himself (Campbell 2017: 519). That Miliband didn't challenge Brown is understandable. The then chancellor had been the presumptive "next leader" since Blair and Brown decided – in disastrously ambiguous terms – that Brown would one day succeed Blair. Yet Miliband had reservations about Brown's (lack of) political agenda (*ibid*.: 520). Their relationship was not a warm one. In the summer of 2008, Miliband wrote an article attacking David Cameron and encouraging the Labour Party to re-energize itself (Miliband 2008). It was an article which, according to Brown, was Miliband "hinting he was ready for a leadership coup" (Brown 2017: 304). For the years of Brown's premiership, the story around David Miliband was "will he or won't he" over challenging Brown, providing a highly scrutinized context for the then foreign secretary's political interventions. Some politicians were less sympathetic to Miliband's position, observing equivocation on the matter of leadership (Wintour 2010).

As the 2010 leadership contest got underway, Ed Miliband gave a media interview which – unsurprisingly – involved confronting his choice to run against his brother. "We're brothers," he said (Stratton & Wintour 2010), "not clones." From 2005 onwards both brothers had been frustrated at the lack of renewal for Labour in office. David Miliband later reflected that New Labour "ultimately ran into the sand because of a failure to adapt, refresh and build on what had been achieved" (2017: 11–12). Yet both had adopted different political stances – and been bestowed different political personas – in the shadow of Blair and Brown. David Miliband was cast as a critic of Brown from the Blairite wing of the party, Ed Miliband as a critic of Blair from the Brownite wing and a loyalist to Brown as prime minister. Because of the overwhelming nature of the global financial crisis in 2008, the final instalment of the New Labour years often seemed a separate, even secondary topic to the years up to 2007; indeed, Brown's role in responding to the global financial meltdown was met with admiration across the party. How to "get over" New Labour jumped back a few years, and – quite reasonably – focused on (Blair's) mistakes. One of the biggest issues that would continue to affect Labour's trajectory for many years was the 2003 decision to invade Iraq.

Today, Tony Blair is chief among a dwindling band of people involved in the decision to go to war who still defend aspects of it. After leaving parliament, David Miliband wrote (*ibid*.: 59–60):

> I voted to support the government's decision to participate in the war … But my assessment of the risks, and therefore my vote, was wrong … It was our – and my – biggest mistake in government. The decision to invade has turned out to be a deep and lasting error, and many Iraqis

are still paying the price ... Of course, when I visit Iraq and discuss its condition, I think about the history. There is only regret.

In 2010, having just vacated government office and been foreign secretary, David Miliband was in a different place on Iraq, only suggesting that it shouldn't play a part in the politics of the leadership race (Batty 2010). He responded defensively to Ed Miliband's very different position (Macintyre 2010), which was broadly to make clear his own opposition to the war (Ed Miliband was not an MP at the time the decision was taken), and argue that more time should have been given to weapons inspectors (looking for weapons of mass destruction) and that the war had led to a "big loss of trust for us" (Wintour & Stratton 2010). This would continue to be an important dividing line in the contest, alongside the more overarching question of New Labour's gradual drift away from the party's core mission.

During the leadership race, David Miliband argued that Labour should not be "scared of ideology, while not getting stuck in dogma" (2010: 41). Ed Miliband, perhaps more comfortable with the language of "ideology", argued that "without values we become managers and technocrats. It is a Labour ideology that makes us who we are" (2010b: 55). Both showed an interest in some of the thinking that became "Blue Labour" – discussed in greater detail in Chapter 2 – which included a similar argument about the lack of a guiding theory (Glasman *et al.* 2011). The difference between the Milibands – articulated on the ground of New Labour's legacy – was over the next project. Ed Miliband projected himself as the candidate who would ditch the New Labour model. "To win next time," he wrote (2010b: 55–6), "it is the New Labour comfort zone that we must escape: the rigidity of old formulae that have served their time, the belittling of any attempt to move on from past verities and the belief that more of the same is the way to win." It was enough for Ed Miliband to win the leadership race, albeit by a very narrow margin. And having won with a mandate for moving on from New Labour, Miliband could return to the arguments he had consistently made since entering politics.

The inequality paradigm

In the early part of 2016, while the then Cameron government geared up for the Brexit referendum which would soon lead to immense political upheaval, Ed Miliband took to the pages of the *London Review of Books* to reflect. He had lost the 2015 general election, which was a shock to him and to many political observers. But he chose to restate his political mission: tackling inequality. What was needed in politics, he wrote, included "much more open discussion about the top 1 per cent". With perhaps one eye on New Labour, he argued (Miliband 2016): "Until quite recently, people would ask why it mattered that those at the top were doing so well, as long as everyone else was prospering too. But it can't any longer be denied that the scale of the rewards reaped by the 1 per cent has the effect of denying others."

The "until quite recently" is important for understanding how Miliband saw the political terrain after the global financial crisis. As Savage argued, after the global financial crisis inequality had become a way of "summarizing a basket of bleak problems ... [linking the] fallout from the austerity politics unleashed across the world in the aftermath of the ... crash to the sense of malaise that was provoked by entrenched and sometimes growing divisions" (2021: 1–2). Politics is often about distribution, even if the politicians doing the politics do not say as much. Part of the inequality paradigm was to refocus the debate on accruing wealth at the top – the "1 per cent" – via the analysis of the economist Joseph Stiglitz and the campaigning of the Occupy protest movement (*ibid.*: 3–7), seeking to highlight and challenge the wealth divide between Wall Street and "Main Street". Ed Miliband recognized the anger early on. About Occupy London, he wrote of "aspects of business, finance and politics which seem in touch with the richest 1% – but badly out of touch with the reality facing the other 99%" (Miliband 2011b).

Comprehending inequality in this way made it "concrete" (Savage 2021: 5), and one can see a similar, powerful effect in the work of the French economist Thomas Piketty. His book, *Capital in the Twenty-First Century* (the English translation of which was first published in 2014), "captured the zeitgeist perfectly" with its focus on the top decile and top percentile relative to the rest of a country's population (Savage 2021: 219; see also Goes 2016: 112; Goldhammer 2017). Piketty remarked, in more recent work, that his methodology did not come with an intention "to replace class warfare with war between the deciles" (2020: 43). Yet he had tapped into a potent construction of the social, political and economic order that different parts of the world experience in different ways. Equality as a political concept – and tackling inequalities of different forms – is of course not a new development on the British left (Jackson 2007). As Freeden noted on equality more broadly, "all socialisms assert the equality of human beings" (1996: 430). I am not contending, therefore, that the "inequality paradigm" introduced Labour to the concept of equality – which would be absurd – nor that there is any simple, causal story here. Rather, the inequality paradigm brought a post-crash emphasis on economic inequality that spoke to Miliband's politics and later to Corbyn's. It encouraged a more critical evaluation of the political past – particularly from the 1980s onwards – and, as Savage noted, it focused more on the inequality problem than the equality ideal (2021: 16). Income inequality in the UK – measured by the Gini coefficient – had stabilized (rather than continued a rapid increase) after the early 1990s, up to when Miliband became leader. Yet it remained "stubbornly above its level in the 1960s and 1970s" (Atkinson 2015: 21). Miliband later wrote that, after the global financial crisis, "those inequalities which had been tolerable when most people's incomes were improving became intolerable" (2021b: 18). This ideological development within the British Labour Party was, then, a part (albeit a small one) of the inequality paradigm story.

What was Piketty's argument? To reiterate, this is not a case of "Ed Miliband read Piketty and he liked it", although both statements are (at least in part, Piketty's books are long) true. Rather, it is that within Piketty's work there are powerful arguments – from detailed analyses of different countries – that demonstrate the political potency of the inequality paradigm, as well as the dilemmas for a politician such as Miliband, seeking to bounce back as the leader of a political party he felt had done too little to change Britain's economy. Savage noted that part of "the challenge of inequality lies in the accumulating force of the weight of history", something which, perhaps lazily, had been assumed to be of less importance in New Labour's heyday (2021: 309), and this is central to Piketty's work. In *Capital*, Piketty presented the time after the world wars and up to 1980 – during which inequality was much reduced – as a period contingent both upon the consequences of war and on the political choices to hold down income and wealth inequality through far higher tax rates than at the very beginning and end of the twentieth century (particularly in Britain and the United States). On this point, Atkinson also noted the centrality of the welfare state in European countries (Atkinson 2015: 75). This period had created an "illusion that the fundamental structural contradiction of capitalism (r>g) had been overcome" (Piketty 2017: 747). That contradiction – r>g – showed that the return on capital was often greater than the growth of economic output (*ibid.*: 746), and it had not been overcome.

Different arguments stemmed from this, and I cannot cover all of them here. The structure of economic inequality had changed since the nineteenth century: there was a large middle class, for example, so wealth was more disbursed (*ibid.*: 532). Other aspects of inequality had made a comeback. The significance of inheritance for a person's life chances was growing (*ibid.*: 481), the largest fortunes experienced the most significant growth (*ibid.*: 561–2) and politicians were once again seeming to take as given the necessity of low tax rates (compared to much of the twentieth century) and meritocratic ideas of an economy that rewarded hard work and potential. Piketty's plan was, broadly and simplistically, to reboot social democracy and to be imaginative in the development of global cooperation to regulate and tax capital (*ibid.*: 663). *Capital* also contained moments of expression for longstanding social democratic or socialist values – and questions – which collided with the politics of the 1990s. For example, Piketty wrote that "every fortune is partially justified yet potentially excessive" (*ibid.*: 562). He reminded people that, if governments did not want to borrow from those who could afford to lend to governments (on the basis of concerns about debt levels), then those same governments could tax the wealthy more (*ibid.*: 739).

In *Capital and Ideology*, the follow-up to *Capital in the Twenty-First Century*, Piketty focused more on the ideological arguments behind equality and inequality. For example, on the political changes of the twentieth century, Piketty noted that "it was the conjunction of two complementary visions of the purpose of taxation (to reduce inequalities and to pay state expenses) that made it possible to transform ownership societies into social-democratic societies" (2020: 462). After the politics of the 1980s, and following on from the picture of society and the global economy presented in *Capital in the Twenty-First Century*, there was surely a moment to confront neoliberalism and conservatism once again (*ibid.*: 570). Ed Miliband had long bought into these kinds of arguments, as we saw earlier with his reflections on ideology towards the end of New Labour. As leader, Miliband wanted to confront both the dominant economic ideas of the last few decades and New Labour's acquiescence in, or even embrace of those ideas. New Labour, he suggested in his first leader's conference speech, had come "to look like a new establishment in the company we kept, the style of our politics and our remoteness from people" (Miliband 2010c). His 2011 speech to conference became known for the language of "predators" and "producers", very clearly targeting a system that New Labour had run and accommodated itself to. Miliband pointed (2011c) to a "crisis":

> It is a crisis of the promises made over the last thirty years. The promise that if you're in work, you will do better each year. The promise that if you work hard at school the doors of opportunity will open up to you … These crises point to something deep in our country. The failure of a system. A way of doing things. An old set of rules.

Such language brings to mind what Piketty called "an inequality regime"; that is, "a set of discourses and institutional arrangements intended to justify and structure the economic, social and political inequalities of a given society" (2020: 2). It was the regime, in its fullness although only seen in parts, that Ed Miliband was aiming at. He found fault in "the way we have chosen to run our country. Not just for a year or so but for decades" (Miliband 2011c). While he suggested that the party should have been "proud" of New Labour's governing achievements, he understood that "good times did not mean we had a good economic system" (*ibid.*). Miliband's alternative was given the name "One Nation" in 2012, and tackling inequality was a part of it: "I will never accept an economy where the gap between rich and poor just grows wider and wider. In One

Nation, in my faith, inequality matters", Miliband said (2012). Moving on from New Labour was necessary because it had failed to hold "those at the top" to their responsibilities (*ibid.*). The message was the same the following year, with a further rhetorical flourish (Miliband 2013b): "They used to say a rising tide lifts all boats, now the rising tide just seems to lift the yachts."

Miliband's final conference speech as leader, in 2014, ended up making headlines for the wrong reasons: he omitted a section on the deficit, then the dominant economic and political issue in British politics, following a consistent Conservative Party message that Labour had overspent in office (see Bale 2015: 250–1). Yet, while he clearly was not succeeding at changing the economic discourse in Britain, he remained consistent in his message (Miliband 2014b): "We just can't carry on with the belief that a country can succeed with a small minority doing well. Prosperity in one part of Britain, among a small elite, a circle that is closed to most, blind to what is going on for everyone but a few."

In a sense, his final conference speech was a snapshot of the strategic dilemma Miliband faced and, at least in part, had contributed to: the pinning on past governments, including New Labour, of the unequal, rigged economy; and a refusal – for perfectly sound and coherent reasons – to accept that New Labour's spending had worsened Britain's economic condition heading into and out of the global financial crisis. For Miliband, New Labour was partly damned by the analysis and ideas contained within the inequality paradigm, yet in the media, it was damned for spending too much money.

Should have been "bolder"

Ed Miliband has since expressed some regrets. "I felt as leader my analysis is big, are the answers big enough?", he said a few years after resigning as Labour leader (Campbell 2018a). A similar refrain came a couple of years after that (Rogers 2021): "I wish I'd been bolder." This gap, or – as Bale put it – this "disjunction … between what some call 'pamphlet Labour' and 'leaflet Labour'" (2015: 264) is encapsulated in the final product: Labour's 2015 manifesto, *Britain Can Be Better*. The manifesto was bookended by some of Miliband's analysis, "problems … mounting for years", and a mention of inequality (Labour Party 2015: 8), to having an economy that currently "might work for some in the City of London but shuts out millions of people in the rest of the country" (*ibid.*: 83). There were policies that spoke to income and wealth inequality, and to inequalities of power and ownership: a 50p top rate of tax, albeit accompanied with the priority of tackling the deficit (*ibid.*: 17); a tax on "mansions" worth over £2 million, with the rhetorical hypothecation of funding for the National Health Service (NHS) (*ibid.*: 18). "Mending" markets had been a key part of Miliband's agenda, and his policy package included a freeze on energy bills, with reform of the sector, and changes to rail ownership processes, including a public sector competitor (*ibid.*: 25–6). A British Investment Bank was to provide support to business as well as co-ops and mutuals (*ibid.*: 21–2).

There was more ambiguity over proposals to "consider how to support employee buy-outs when businesses are being sold", along with reforms to executive pay (*ibid.*: 21). There was intent, but the manifesto sought above all to minimize perceived negatives for Labour. Priority was instead given to dealing with "legacy issues" – particularly spending – without conceding the economic argument, all the while not fully committing to Miliband's instinctive alternative. This takes us back to the dilemma Miliband struggled with: he wanted to move on from New Labour, and that involved a big critique of British politics going back decades, including the New Labour years. He also thought that New Labour's spending was not something to be attacked, but his defence was made in the shadow of an overarching critique. This fostered a sense of unease among some New Labour figures, for example Alastair Campbell, who talked and met with Miliband during this time. He recorded in his diary (2021: 438):

> Ed came round … he did not agree about my message on his approach to the past. He felt he has to have distance between himself and the TB-GB records. I felt we had to have in people's minds a sense that at least when Labour was in power, we got stuff done, but he was not buying it. I felt we had conceded way too much, that we had played into the Tories' line of attack on the whole financial mess being of our making.

Targeting an "inequality regime" made criticism of New Labour's role inevitable. Yet Miliband's strategy, while intellectually coherent, was hard to deliver. *Britain Can Be Better* spoke to the rather tortuous process of attempting to reconcile Miliband's beliefs with the reluctance of others to criticize New Labour, and with the admonishments of focus groups regarding New Labour's record on spending. Yet the core idea – that there was an alternative economic model and that Labour had accommodated itself far too much and too often to a pre-existing one – was critical to the project that came after Miliband too.

Anti-austerity

When Jeremy Corbyn announced that he would be running for the Labour leadership, to his local party and newspaper on 3 June 2015, the response focused on the likelihood that his candidacy would "widen the debate"; indeed, that was part of the reason Corbyn said he was running (Gayle 2015). Owen Jones, writing soon afterwards (2015) appealed, "come on, Labour MPs. Put your future careers aside for party and national interest. Lend Corbyn a nomination, and let a real debate begin." On the BBC's *Newsnight* programme a few days later, Corbyn was asked whether, with his background as a "rebel" backbencher on Labour's left for decades, he was "someone who's happy to be … in the wilderness, against the entire mainstream?" (BBC 2015). That Corbyn's ascent to be Labour leader was a surprise to many is an obvious point. But it is an important one for understanding what his leadership meant for Labour's ideology after Miliband. What became "Corbynism" was an interesting mix of Labour traditions and ideas, with meanings contingent upon Corbyn and the political moment itself. It was not a ready-to-go alternative to Miliband and was squarely located within the inequality paradigm. On the subject of Labour's 2015 manifesto, Corbyn said he had "agreed with most of it … the problem was the fundamental economic strategy was not that different" to the Conservatives (*ibid.*).

An unambiguous anti-austerity stance animated the early Corbyn campaign, along with a big distinction from defenders of the New Labour years: the repudiation of the Iraq War (Pike & Diamond 2021: 675–6). In his first article for *The Guardian* launching his candidacy, Corbyn stressed both themes (2015a), alongside an emphasis on inequality. He argued that the leadership election should "be more aspirational about closing the huge inequality gap in Britain", and on foreign policy he suggested (*ibid.*): "There has also long been a peace tradition within Labour, much of which was suppressed, if not forced to disappear, under New Labour." Corbyn's campaign was, in many ways, Miliband's analysis accompanied by an amnesty on all fears of media or public scepticism about policy answers. Corbyn became the figurehead for a movement created around him and parts of his backstory, opposition to the Iraq War being a key part of it. That movement had a great deal of policy and campaigning energy, which swiftly took Corbyn to the front of the leadership pack and a resounding triumph in the leadership race. It was his lack of hesitancy, and clarity in opposing austerity, that appeared to be so refreshing.

How fair was the "austerity-lite" criticism applied to Miliband and his shadow chancellor, Ed Balls? Labour's 2015 manifesto had noted that "outside of the protected areas of health, education and international development there will be cuts in spending" (Labour Party 2015: 17). Yet following an analysis of the parties' plans for the public finances during the 2015 election campaign, the deputy director of the Institute for Fiscal Studies, Carl Emmerson, pointed to a big difference between the Conservatives and Labour: the former required "substantial and almost entirely unspecified spending cuts and tax increases" to meet their plans. Labour's plan, meanwhile, was more ambiguous, and may have entailed "little in the way of spending cuts" after the first year (Institute for Fiscal Studies 2015). That Ed Miliband wasn't shouting this from the rooftops can be explained by concerns over the public perception of the party. Polling suggested the Conservatives remained ahead on being trusted to run the economy (Jordan 2015), and Miliband's *Question Time* performance during the final part of the election campaign saw some parts of the media focusing on spending and Labour's record (Sweney 2015). Corbyn's campaign – and subsequent political project – was defining itself more against Ed Miliband's hesitant and cautious political strategy than any real "austerity-lite" programme.

"It's called socialism"

"Rampant inequality has become the great scandal of our time", Corbyn told the party's 2016 annual conference. It was "sapping the potential of our society and tearing at its fabric. Labour's goal isn't just greater equality of wealth and income, but also of power" (Corbyn 2016). As with Miliband's rhetoric, this politics can be located within the inequality paradigm; that is, a moment in time partly defined by the challenge of inequality and new forms of understanding. There were key differences, however, with the Miliband period: that Labour would be interventionist on the economy – and "unapologetic" about it – rather than displaying the hesitancy of the Miliband years (Corbyn 2015c); and that Labour would enthusiastically build out from the analysis contained within the inequality paradigm, endorsing a multitude of policy ideas. Corbyn himself, unlike Miliband, was not the main driver of the project's ideology: Corbynism or, with the political economy focus, "Corbynomics". Where Miliband was often his own ideological engine, Corbyn has been described by supportive thinkers as an example of a "servant-leader", putting into effect the "demands" of a movement (Berry & Guinan 2019: 24–5). John McDonnell in particular embraced the movement for alternative economic ideas. He brought in well-known analysts of inequality – Stiglitz and Piketty – alongside Mariana Mazzucato, Simon Wren-Lewis (author of influential blogs about austerity) and Danny Blanchflower as part of an "advisory panel" (Peston 2015). He often appeared proud of novel ideological clarity, conviction and commitment to left tradition: a riposte to the years of New Labour. As he told conference delegates, "in this party you no longer have to whisper it, it's called socialism" (McDonnell 2016).

"Past shadow chancellors", McDonnell later argued (2018c), "have come to conference with warnings about how bad the situation is to reduce people's expectations of what can be achieved when we go into government. This shadow chancellor is different." The strategic ambiguity, and the reasoned warnings to prevent accusations of profligacy seen in previous years, was the target here. The result of these two key differences with the Miliband leadership – the lack of hesitancy and the willingness to embrace many ideas that built out from the analysis of the inequality paradigm – saw a period of political and policy ferment. According to one sympathetic observer, this was in contrast to *later* New Labour, where political energy, however naïve or wrong-headed, had given way to politicians who "sound like dull building society managers" (Seymour 2016: 142). It was this managerialism that Blairites and New Labour were often associated with after 2010. Corbynism was very far from managerial. Miliband had targeted Labour's predilection for confusing "ideology" with "dogmatism". The Corbyn project added a further difference from New Labour: an unflinching style of socialist politics, free of the "professionalism" which had become a symbol of New Labour's perceived inauthenticity.

Corbyn's leadership was tumultuous from day one, as is well known. Within a year of Corbyn winning the leadership, Conservative Prime Minister David Cameron had resigned after losing the referendum on Britain's membership of the EU. The result was devastating for Labour too, having been committed to the European project since the "modernization" period of the 1980s. Corbyn was swiftly criticized by his own party for a perceived lack of campaigning passion – and interest – during the referendum (Asthana 2016). A spate of shadow cabinet resignations was followed by a confidence vote of the parliamentary party – which Corbyn lost by 172 votes to 40 (Asthana *et al.* 2016). Cameron used the prime minister's questions session in the week after the referendum to call for Corbyn to quit (Hansard HC Deb, 29 June 2016). The parliamentary party succeeded in triggering a contest, with Owen Smith – then Labour MP for Pontypridd – emerging as the challenger to Corbyn. Smith was swiftly labelled the "Blair-lite" candidate by sources speaking to the media (Asthana & Elgot 2016). The contest saw Corbyn secure a slightly bigger mandate than the already sizeable one he achieved in 2015 (Dorey & Denham 2016), yet the campaign included some insights into the future, such as Smith's call for a confirmatory referendum (of some sort) or election regarding a future Brexit deal.

Despite the chaos within Labour, and in part because of it, Corbynism was fleshed out quickly. By the time of the leader's 2016 conference speech, big-ticket policies – such as a National Investment Bank and a National Education Service – were already announced. By this point, Theresa May was the new Conservative prime minister, and the party was looking ahead to a general election. This came along fast, after May made a statement in Downing Street in April 2017. The result – a much stronger Labour performance than many commentators had expected – was critical to how Corbynism came to be seen and how it developed further. As two political scientists put it (Cowley & Kavanagh 2018: 413): "Labour won the campaign; it did not win the election." Corbyn was not prime minister, but Labour's anti-austerity frame appeared to have struck a chord (*ibid.*: 424). It was a victory against expectations; one which carried the danger of feeling like a victory full stop, which it was not. Theresa May was lampooned as the "Maybot" on account of her robotic style and lack of political flexibility (Crace 2017). Corbyn's project, on the other hand, seemed to have forged a connection with people. It was popular, if not victorious, and a genuine alternative.

There was much focus on the 2017 manifesto (which I detail below). May's policy offer had been a high-profile disaster. Labour's, closely bound up with the Corbyn project's political outlook (Cowley & Kavanagh 2018: 437), seemed to have shifted the electoral dial. Corbynism became, after 2017, a project that was increasingly confident of the approach I described above: unflinching in its ambition and building out from the inequality paradigm with even more ideas. There is a divide, among observers of the party – including academics – about just how "radical" the 2017 manifesto was. Jackson, a historian of political ideas, argued that the manifesto offered "a fairly conventional social democratic politics", which many had queried the health of after the 2010 turn to austerity (Jackson 2017: 343). Others pushed back on this, arguing instead that the 2017 manifesto had "the seeds of a radical transformation beyond social democracy", particularly with its focus on ownership (Berry & Guinan 2019: 34). Much of this depends on the frame of reference. Viewing "social democracy" as a political tradition over the last century, Labour's 2017 manifesto was certainly recognizably within that tradition. Yet it is also true to say, as Cowley and Kavanagh did, that it marked the most obviously left policy programme for Labour since 1983 (2018: 184).

Understood through the argument presented in this chapter, it marked the moment where Labour's ideology – now firmly located within the analysis of the inequality paradigm – shook off some of the hesitancy of the Miliband period, particularly when it came to tax and spend. Additional day-to-day spending of £48.6 billion would be funded through tax measures, with borrowing funding investment (Labour Party 2017b: 4–5). There would be a £250 billion National Transformation Fund, investing that cash over ten years (Labour Party 2017a: 11). There were ambitious plans for public services, including laying "the foundations of a National Care Service for England" (*ibid*.: 71) and stopping Sure Start centre (children's centres) closures, with more money for the New Labour flagship scheme (*ibid*.: 36). The National Education Service and a National Investment Bank, referred to above, were included too, the latter involving a plan to raise private capital (*ibid*.: 16). The emerging "ownership" plans included public ownership of rail, utilities and Royal Mail, a "right to own", giving employees the chance to buy a company they work for if it is being sold (*ibid*.: 19) and a reference to local procurement (*ibid*.: 14). The latter was associated with the so-called Preston model: a set of policies being pursued by Preston's Labour-run council which sought to change the local economic context.

Matthew Brown, a Labour councillor and leader of Preston council, described the strategy (in a book co-authored with Rhian E. Jones) as "shifting spending and investment from external suppliers to local producers and businesses … [building] strategic alliances with local anchor institutions … [and] towards a model that supports community wealth-building, collective ownership and democratic participation" (2021: 45).

The NHS, as a major local employer across the different nations of the UK, can be understood as an "anchor institution". A local NHS can – and should, through this thinking – spend more of its necessary outgoings in the local area (*ibid.*: 51). The point about collective ownership relates to both demand and supply: that if demand can be met locally, it should be met locally, and if can't be, then attempts should be made at creating collectively owned suppliers for that demand. Here, the focus includes co-operatives, inspired by examples from around the world (*ibid.*: 49). This is part of the challenge – in the words of Berry and Guinan – to a neoliberal "extractive" economic approach, where "elites extract and monopolize wealth and power through their ownership of resources that should serve the common good" (2019: 18). Affecting property and ownership relations can change this model, with more wealth retained in communities. There were two major parts of Corbynomics, one of which was still developing in 2017: big ambitions to tax, spend and borrow to invest, all "traditional" social democratic methods, including within contemporary social democracy; and then plans to change property and ownership relations, with a shift of power from – to use the language of the inequality paradigm – the 1 per cent to the rest.

McDonnell summarized the approach in a lecture to the Marx Memorial Library. He used the word "renaissance" in relation to the plethora of ideas coming from Labour at the time. The mission, in McDonnell's words, was a "radically fairer, radically more democratic, radically more equal [society] … a socialist society" (McDonnell 2018b). The approach involved tax reform and spending for a fairer and more equal society, investment to create opportunity and wealth and institutional change to bring about a more democratic (and, again, more equal) society (*ibid.*). The latter was termed the "institutional turn" by supportive thinkers, again focused on the plans around ownership (Guinan & O'Neill 2018). The year 2018 saw the Corbyn project furnished with more big policies which spoke to the inequality paradigm: inequalities of income, wealth and power. It was Theresa May's last full year as prime minister, as she battled – in vain – to secure Conservative backbench support for a Brexit deal that Eurosceptics would continue to reject. Corbyn, McDonnell and their allies could continue to look back at the electoral surprise of 2017 with confidence, and continue in asserting the importance of moving on from New Labour. For example, in the introduction of a book on Corbynomics that he edited, McDonnell wrote

(2018a: ix): "For decades, successive governments have told us that free markets were always best and private wealth should be left untouched. They 'rolled back the frontiers of the state' and were 'seriously relaxed about people becoming filthy rich' ... Yet wealth today piles up in a few hands and insecure work is at record levels."

Note the "they" which joins together the famous quote from Margaret Thatcher and an equally famous comment from Peter Mandelson, although Mandelson is usually quoted as having said "intensely" rather than "seriously" relaxed. The line being drawn between contemporary Labour and New Labour – one firmly about inequality – was obvious.

McDonnell headlined his interventions over the 2018 conference period with changes to business ownership and a shift of economic power towards workers and the state (Helm 2018). "Inclusive ownership funds" formed a key part of Labour's economic reforms, with employees as a group owning up to 10 per cent of a large company, gradually accrued, and worth up to £500 per year, per worker (Labour Party 2019a: 60). The £500 figure was a cap, with any excess collected by the state to fund a "Climate Apprenticeship Fund", although this new kind of tax was also limited at 25 per cent of funds generated by the employee shares (*ibid.*). Labour went into the 2019 general election with a bigger, bolder and more confident version of its answer to the challenges exposed through the inequality paradigm. The 2019 "greybook" of costings for its proposals increased current spending by £82.9 billion, with the claim of tax-raising measures to match the spends (Labour Party 2019b: 4–5). That was around £35 billion more than pledged in 2017. Capital spending pledges were bolstered too. There was a £400 billion National Transformation Fund, £250 billion of which was earmarked for green investment (Labour Party 2019a: 13). The other £150 billion would "replace, upgrade, and expand our schools, hospitals, care homes and council houses" (*ibid.*: 30). Sure Start closures wouldn't only be stopped, as in 2017. Instead, Labour committed to "reverse cuts to Sure Start and create a new service, Sure Start Plus, with enough centres to provide a genuinely universal service, available in all communities" (*ibid.*: 38).

According to one account of the Corbyn years, the 2019 manifesto "amounted to Corbynism on steroids in the eyes of the media" (Pogrund & Maguire 2020: 316). Media coverage focused on tax and spend commitments – in particular, a proposal to provide free broadband services (Walker *et al.* 2019). The boldness of the offer can be seen, at least in part, as an attempt to "change the conversation" of the election from Brexit to big, bold domestic policies. With May having been replaced by Boris Johnson, and with Westminster having entered a black hole of Brexit politics, the election was framed (successfully) by the Conservatives as being about leaving the EU. Labour's divisions had worsened, with the Corbyn leadership eventually acceding to a policy of a referendum on a "Labour Brexit deal" versus remaining in the EU, something I discuss in more detail in Chapter 2. Corbyn tried, in his rhetoric, to insist that the inequality paradigm trumped Brexit divides (where 52 per cent of UK voters had backed leaving the EU), returning to a symbol of post-crash politics: "A Labour government will transform our economy and communities. We stand not just for the 52 per cent or the 48 per cent but for the 99 per cent", he declared (Corbyn 2019). Divides over the former won out.

Mission statement

Keir Starmer won the campaign to succeed Jeremy Corbyn with a continuity platform. Starmer said that New Labour had "strayed too far from its values between 1997 and 2010", singling out Iraq and inequality (Williams & Stewart 2019). Among Starmer's "10 pledges" as a candidate were commitments to "economic justice" – including an increase in "income tax for the top 5% of earners" – and "common ownership of rail, mail, energy and water" (Starmer Leadership Campaign 2020). Candidate Starmer's language was steeped in the inequality paradigm (Starmer 2020): "Today's inequalities and injustices are obvious: a radical Labour government is needed now more than ever. Inequalities of every type – in power, education, health and wealth – have become ingrained in our society."

Starmer had "made clear from the off that the bulk of the Corbynite economic programme would remain intact" (Pogrund & Maguire 2020: 338). And yet it has not. Why? In part it is because Starmer has been fleshing out a political identity while learning how to be a leader of the opposition. He has been trying to find an ideological space in and around the Labour Party that he feels comfortable in, and has changed his mind a lot. Elected in 2015, Starmer was seen as broadly "soft left" and highly competent, but there was little to point to on political definition. This can be an asset for an ambitious politician. As shadow Brexit secretary under Corbyn, Starmer – very gradually – came to adopt a narrow, anti-Brexit political identity. He partnered this in the leadership election with continuity on Corbynomics and the pre-existing "moving on from New Labour" message, which worked well for him. Yet he swiftly began searching for something else. In Chapter 3, I consider in much more detail Starmer's willingness to adopt political positions, drop them and then adopt others. Here I focus on where he has landed, ideologically, with a technocratic understanding of missions thinking in the context of the Labour leader's shifting priorities.

Starmer's path to finding a political narrative for his leadership has been convoluted, although, it should be noted, his leadership began in turbulent times, with the onset of the Covid-19 pandemic. In a speech, titled "A New Chapter for

Britain", delivered early in 2021, Starmer channelled a "1945 moment", noting a "mood in the air which we don't detect often in Britain" (Starmer 2021a), owing to the pandemic emergency and the spotlight that had been shone on longstanding inequalities. Jump forwards seven months and Starmer had published a Fabian Society pamphlet (Starmer 2021b) ahead of his 2021 Labour conference address which, while unobjectionable to many, was banal and lacked definition. When Boris Johnson's leadership first began its descent into crisis after the "partygate" revelations – gatherings at Number 10 Downing Street occurring during Covid restrictions – Starmer found a sense of political purpose, contrasting his record of public service with a prime minister increasingly viewed as unserious and unsuitable for the job. When Liz Truss occupied Number 10 for a month and a half in 2022, Starmer again found purpose through reacting to his opponent. His 2022 conference speech was the most ideologically certain since his leadership campaign, condemning Truss for (short-lived) "tax cuts for the richest 1% in our society. Don't forget. Don't forgive" (Starmer 2022). With Truss presenting the most overtly ideological Conservatism for some time, Starmer felt comfortable attacking "trickle-down economics". "Britain won't be better off", he argued, "just because we make the rich, richer" (*ibid.*).

After Truss's replacement with Rishi Sunak, Starmer opted to contest, for the most part, in the political space of competency and management. Anxious about the market response to the "mini budget" of Truss and her chancellor, Kwasi Kwarteng – and conscious of the tired but repeated Conservative mantra of Labour overspending – Starmer's Labour shifted emphasis once again. This is particularly clear on the issue of taxation. In a speech to the 2021 Labour conference, the shadow chancellor Rachel Reeves set out some principles for tax and spend. She said (Reeves 2021):

> Good public services have to be paid for. But how we pay for them is a test of our values. Today I want to share the principles that underlie our approach to taxation. First, we will make the tax system fairer, ensuring that the burden isn't just falling on the wages of working people, but that those at the top pay their fair share too.

Reeves contrasted the tax paid on income by a public sector worker to the tax paid "by someone making many times more from buying and selling stocks and shares" and who pays capital gains tax. "This will not stand with Labour", she declared (*ibid.*). The Institute for Public Policy Research – a think tank – picked up on this at the time, welcoming the direction taken (IPPR 2021). Yet less than two years later, with Labour campaigning for votes ahead of the 2023 local elections – at which they picked up more than 500 council seats – Reeves chose not to reiterate this. Asked specifically about capital gains tax, the shadow chancellor told the BBC's *Today* programme that she had no plans to increase it (BBC 2023a). Starmer took an even more cautious – and conservative – line in the run-up to those same elections. Asked specifically about his 2020 leadership pledge to increase taxes on the top 5 per cent of earners, the Labour leader responded that "we" were in a "different situation".

Pointing to the increasing figure of tax as a share of gross domestic product (GDP) – what he (along with many others) called the "tax burden" – Starmer said (2023g):

> If they've [the Conservatives] proved one thing, it's that their high tax, low growth economy doesn't work … I think it's busted … my answer on what we do about the economy is we've got to grow the economy. I accept … I'm giving you a different answer to, perhaps, previous Labour leaders which would always go straight to tax and spend.

In a separate interview with *The Economist* around the same time, Starmer emphasized – apparently in an attempt at reassurance – that Labour wanted to avoid increases in taxation, denying any reform plans for capital gains tax in particular. He told the magazine (Starmer 2023f):

> I accept the proposition that the tax burden is higher now than I think it has been at any stage for I don't know how many years … I resist the idea that the first place you go is tax … the instinct is always to think that's where Labour wants to go first, and it isn't because we've got to get economic growth … Quite often we're challenged on capital-gains tax. We don't have plans, actually, on capital gains tax. It's important that I make that clear. But I, and Rachel, intend to resist the pull that so many people urge on us that the first place a Labour government goes is to tax. The first place the next Labour government will go is to grow.

Starmer did mention three specific tax changes that Labour planned, all broadly in the area of high income and wealth: changing "non-dom" tax status so that non-domiciled tax advantages are reduced, scrapping a tax exemption for private schools and taxing those working in private equity at a higher rate. Labour has also committed to extending a windfall tax scheme for energy firms.

On Starmer's unease about the "tax burden", and his use of this measure to move away from his "top 5 per cent" pledge, it is the case that tax revenue as a share of GDP was forecast to reach a 70-year-high (Bell *et al.* 2023). Yet it is a more complex picture than is sometimes suggested, both in terms of novelty and causation. First, rising UK taxes as a share of GDP was a topic of debate on the public policy agenda prior to Starmer's commitment to raise taxes for the highest earners (Corlett 2019). Second, the tax as a share of GDP figure is the product of different factors, including, for example, inequality or changes to the structure of the UK economy over decades (*ibid.*: 5). Third, according to data from the Institute for Fiscal Studies' TaxLab, there have been significant moves in the share of GDP figure before, including from 1993–4 to 2000–1, where it increased from 28.4 per cent to 33.3 per cent (IFS 2021). Fourth, and more specifically about Starmer's 2020 pledge on higher earners, work looking at more recent changes in personal taxation suggested that tax rises in 2023–4 for the highest-income households represented just over 1 per cent of their income (Corlett 2023: 8). I return to the topic of tax, and what Labour's policy should be, in Chapter 4. The important point for now is that debates about tax are more complex than Starmer has suggested. They involve political judgements about distribution, and about what tax is used for and why a country needs it. Any dilemmas encountered while forming a view are not resolved by the data Starmer alluded to.

Labour has produced distinctive policy ideas outside of taxation, including over £20 billion in green investment over a parliament. This was a downgrade from the £28 billion a year Ed Miliband – back in the shadow cabinet and leading on climate – had fought for and defended, in part through doling out praise to his colleagues (Miliband 2023). The party's "New Deal for Working People" addressed inequality and offered policies that would boost the power of organized labour. Such policy work is in the realm of "predistribution"; that is, seeking to affect economic outcomes *pre* distribution and redistribution through the welfare system (see Goes 2021: 186–90 for a discussion of the meanings related to this term). The package committed to the eradication of "in-work poverty", strengthening collective bargaining through "fair pay agreements" across some sectors of the economy, introducing protections from "remote surveillance" technologies, removing recently established obstacles to trade union organizing and industrial action, and outlawing "fire and rehire" practices that seek to worsen a worker's terms and conditions (Labour Party 2022b). In Chapter 2, I look at the party's commitment to decentralization and giving more economic freedoms to local authorities.

An agenda has cohered – something I consider in more detail in Chapter 4 – although, partly on the basis of people's experience of Starmer's leadership, much Labour policy has a "provisional" aura: from the amount of money committed, to the timing and detail of regulatory changes. Labour's industrial strategy and its green commitments are mutually reinforcing, and both speak to the decentralization agenda, as well as creating better, well-paid jobs with enhanced employment rights. These connections – leading to shared policy objectives across different policy areas – have duly formed a significant part of Starmer's "mission-driven government" narrative (Starmer 2023c); an approach to politics that he has appeared comfortable with. With Labour having set out some missions for the party's industrial strategy (Labour Party 2022a), this concept was put front and centre by Starmer in 2023. For the Labour leader, missions provided a longer-term focus, breaking from what he called "sticking plaster" politics (Starmer 2023c). He was taken by the notion of setting objectives that encourage government and the private sector to work towards common goals, as well as loosening central government's grip on how policy is developed and implemented (*ibid.*). Starmer set out five such missions: achieving the "highest sustained growth in the G7", with a stress on growth all over the UK and on creating good jobs; making Britain a "clean energy superpower", with the key detail of "zero-carbon electricity by 2030"; having an NHS "fit for the future", with a focus on reform and speeding things up; safe streets, with a focus on preventing violence against women and girls; and finally the commitment to "break down the barriers to opportunity at every stage", with a rather vague notion of early years and education reform (Labour Party 2023a), somewhat fleshed out with the rhetoric of smashing Britain's "class ceiling" (Labour Party 2023d).

Starmer followed up his speech with an essay for the *New Statesman*, where he noted the work of Mariana Mazzucato, an economist with experience of devising missions in public policy. Starmer defined the concept in a way related to Mazzucato's work, arguing that missions could "galvanize all parts of government and civil society and provide focus" (Starmer 2023d). In response to Starmer's essay, Mazzucato cautiously welcomed Starmer's revival of a missions approach, while making some observations. Mazzucato noted (2023), for example, that Labour's NHS mission would be better focused on health outcomes rather than on the goal of reform. And aiming for the highest sustained growth in the G7, meanwhile, would "be better defined as a policy priority" rather than a mission (*ibid.*). It is on this point that Starmer's understanding of missions thinking revealed his continued lack of a guiding ideology. To be a mission in the way Mazzucato described, the economic objective would need to be partnered with a clearer political economy. For example, and to return to Piketty's thinking, that could mean wrestling with the growing inequalities within contemporary capitalism and the accrual of wealth at the top. In short, missions thinking is not a substitute for an ideology, neither conceptually or politically. It does not tell you, for instance, what kind of growth to aim for.

When Starmer said that "Starmerism is as much about the 'how' as the 'what'" (Starmer 2023f), he was speaking to some of the insight that can no doubt be taken from missions thinking for the goal of state reform. And the objective of getting government working again is a perfectly admirable goal. However, Mazzucato's missions thinking was as much values-led as state reforming. Economic growth, she wrote, "has not only a rate but also a direction – and that direction should have purpose" (2021: 168). That purpose – for Mazzucato

– should be reforming capitalism, making it greener, less focused on finance and more focused on what she called "the 'creation of public value'" rather than rent seeking (*ibid.*: 169). Starmer certainly acknowledged that part of missions thinking was shaping markets; in other words, deciding on a policy priority and seeking to create a market that helps deliver that, rather than accommodating to existing markets (Starmer 2023c). More high-quality jobs and growth across the UK – not only in London and the south-east – alongside policies to boost workers' rights and to decentralize power and money could, with the right investment, act as market-shaping objectives. But a growth target does not represent a clear ideological guide for a Labour government, outside of certain policy areas: for instance planning reform.

In Chapter 3, I discuss in greater depth Starmer's political identity crisis and his motivations for wholly committing to one policy agenda and then skipping to another. Times do change. That Starmer became leader during the pandemic crisis and has served as leader of the opposition during another – Russia's invasion of Ukraine – is relevant to his context and his decision-making. The reason that I focus so much in this chapter on taxation speaks, however, to a separate and significant lack of a guiding ideology. A diagnosis of "strategic ambiguity" would be much too generous to characterize moving from principles of fairer taxation – including pledges to increase taxation on higher earners – to doubling down on having few plans on personal taxation at all. Starmer has not been quiet on tax, he has been ruling things out. The (admittedly turbulent) context has not made a change of heart inevitable either. Instead, the diagnosis is of a Labour leadership that doesn't yet know what it wants to achieve with office. Starmer knows he wants to be prime minister, and that clearly matters, although I discuss different motivations for that goal in Chapter 3. And Starmer is at his most convincing when talking about running the institutions of the British state, because he has, after all, already run a public service. On what Starmer wants to do with power, he is yet to have fully decided. In government, being "reactive" is a double-edged sword. Labour will need a clearer sense of ideological purpose.

Conclusion

Labour's ideological journey since the end of New Labour has been an interesting one. For some, it may appear to have been confusing. How did Labour go from the party of Blair to the party of Corbyn in less than a decade? Was it a trip back to the 1980s, to Labour's comfort zone, or to populism? My argument in this chapter is that much of the change since 2010 is only comprehensible when understanding people's motivations: chiefly the motivation of turning away from how New Labour had come to be seen, within a wider context of political change in other countries too. Ed Miliband took aim at New Labour's acquiescence (at best) within an economic system that was failing the many and rewarding the few. As he has since recognized, his reading of the political and economic world was impactful, his policy platform less so. In part, this was because of doubts about whether dumping on New Labour would see the party swiftly returned to power. Miliband's analysis led to a dilemma: how to represent change while defending parts of New Labour's record and restoring public trust in Labour's competence. He did not succeed.

Corbyn, unlike Miliband, was far from being his own ideological engine. Ideas poured into the Corbyn project, and that wasn't by accident or because Corbyn was uninterested; it was part of the idea of his leadership. The analysis Corbynism represented was less novel than is often thought. What was different was the willingness to embrace – at scale – a policy platform that spoke to the analysis. There is no one "lesson" to take from this approach, because Corbyn's leadership saw two very different election results: one that defied expectations and one that devastated Labour's standing. In Chapters 2 and 3 I discuss how Corbynism fell apart in the face of Brexit. Having walked away from his opening continuity platform, it has been easy to portray Starmer as following a New Labour playbook. There certainly has been a counter-reaction, ideologically, to aspects of the Miliband and Corbyn years. And some Labour political actors – for example, the shadow health secretary Wes Streeting – are fond of rekindling rhetoric and policy associated with later New Labour. But the main takeaway in relation to Starmerism is the lack of consistency and of clarity. Labour often has plenty of policies, but what it wants to achieve – which should be guided by a clearly articulated ideology – has been subject to numerous, swift changes since 2019. The conclusion that Labour is unclear about what it wants is, for now, unavoidable.

2
DEMOCRACY: KNOCKING ON DOORS AND CHANGING THE WORLD

Introduction

The Labour Party is, quite often, in a state of what the Italian political scientist Giovanni Sartori once termed "democratic confusion" (1987: 72). Democracy, as Charles Taylor set out (2022: 19), is in part a telic concept: in short, a values-led political effort that may never be fully realized (Calhoun 2022: 48). As such, some in and around the Labour Party are restless for a democratic politics of greater participation and cooperation: building solidarity and democratic practices that can survive electoral ups and downs. After the Blair and Brown years, the party had withered as a democratic force. It had lost a general election, of course, and needed to rebuild a relationship with the electorate. Yet that was not the only sign of decay. The party had, it was argued, ceased to be a "movement". Richard Sennett wrote of a divide on the political left between "top-down" and "bottom-up" approaches to solidarity (2013: 39). In other words, a bureaucracy at the top dispensing social justice, or grassroots campaigning demanding and sometimes enacting change from below. The Labour Party has both traditions within it, and wrestling with this conceptual difficulty can be productive. As is often the case, both traditions have a role to play. The fear after the New Labour years was that the party had become all top down, squeezing out bottom-up creativity and renewal.

Labour activists have long believed in an organizational mission of being rooted in communities, and for much of the twentieth century there was a clear expression of this through the organized working class, the institutions working people built and the construction of shared narratives (Lawrence 2020). The party's origins in trade unionism mean "the party" and "the movement", Labour and labour, have a longstanding democratic relationship. It has never been an uncomplicated one, and it remains key. But being in the business of minimizing the gap between those who govern and the governed now requires new efforts and new ideas, in no small part because of economic and social changes, with the superseding of traditional measures of class and a smaller trade union movement. New Labour began with aspirations to be a "mass party", in part to respond to these changes. It ended with a reduced membership, a reputation for control freakery and "centralization", and images that defined its political approach, such as Walter Wolfgang, an octogenarian Labour Party member, being removed from the party conference hall for an anti-war heckle (Jones 2005). If Labour exists in part to challenge how politics is conducted (the "rules of the game") – which it surely does – then by the end of New Labour, the perception was largely of a party that existed to uphold the status quo, ignore dissent and maintain a certain distance.

To get over New Labour meant the party becoming a "movement" again and letting go of power in multiple ways. Making that happen, however, was and is complicated. Unlike the Conservative Party, Labour aspires to be a democratic organization; in other words, how the party takes decisions (and who takes them) is a product of a constantly changing "microdemocracy" (Sartori 1987: 11). The role of the party in our democracy is in part a product of how it is run. However, while I refer to some changes in the party's internal democracy, my focus here is not on the arcana of Labour's rule book (a relief I'm sure). Rather, this chapter shows how – after 2010 – successive Labour people, including its leaders, turned towards movement politics (Avril 2019). The story takes in very different factions – including Blue Labour and Momentum – as well as some singular moments, such as Ed Miliband at an early morning fish market and Jeremy Corbyn onstage at Glastonbury. What these all have in common is a faith in democracy as "people's power" (Geuss 2001: 113). Democracy is understood not only as judgement and authorization at the ballot box – either at general or local elections – but as a process of participation, deliberation and meeting the demands of the people, all of the time.

This response to New Labour did not mean the party was immune to reading the temperature of the United Kingdom through focus groups and opinion polls. Rather, if New Labour was *only* about those methods, Labour now had to reconnect with some different ones and push back against what were seen as New Labour practices and tendencies. That meant local Labour parties being driven by local demands and campaigns rather than parroting national campaign lines and treating voters as consumers. If Labour Party meetings were famous for extended discussions about the minutes of the previous meeting, and known for being off-putting, enthusiasm-sapping gatherings, they needed to be revamped as opportunities for political and policy debates. More ambitiously, Labour needed to embrace a different model of political leadership: one where social movements could provide the "social" political lead, with Labour adding its "electoral" and "parliamentary" political weight; and one where more people would participate in democratic deliberation and decision-making. From

Miliband to Corbyn, the story is of reacting to New Labour's legacy but failing to realize the ambitions of both leaders and activists alike. Ed Miliband's embrace of "community organizing" – made famous, at the time, by the early career of US President Barack Obama and the activists involved in his own presidential campaigns – was short-lived. For Jeremy Corbyn, change was much more noticeable, both through huge numbers of new party members and the profile of Momentum, the campaign group that sprang from his 2015 leadership campaign. Yet for those involved, the consensus was of another failure to realize early ambitions. The Brexit dilemma was a huge test for Corbyn's "new politics", and the latter ultimately unravelled when confronted with the former.

Under Keir Starmer's leadership, the party has appeared to ditch much of the reflection on "becoming a movement again". Is it easily dismissed as a distraction from winning general elections. Yet while Starmer has shown limited interest in some of the ideas from the Miliband and Corbyn periods, he has paid significant attention to reforming the UK's democracy if Labour wins office, pledging to devolve power and chastising a broken Westminster system (Starmer 2023a). This, I argue, makes Labour thinking about social movements – and how to change as a political party – even more important. In recent years, people-powered social movements have made a big impact, from Black Lives Matter and climate activism to campaigns against male violence. There is also a relatively resurgent trade unionism in the context of a cost-of-living crisis – centred around people such as Mick Lynch of the National Union of Rail, Maritime and Transport Workers (RMT) – that aspires to the kind of movement politics some in the Corbyn project had hoped to coincide with.

On this, Labour's approach has been circumspect. Labour is committed to a programme of political decentralization and has influential political figures who want Labour to trust people with power. Yet some continue to place an emphasis on the importance of control and distance from grassroots campaigning. In a host of areas, not least in how the party engages with communities, these two political approaches clash. Since 2010, either through party reform or commitments to constitutional change, Labour has moved towards more participatory ideas for our democracy (Sartori 1987: 113–16), but debates and big choices remain. Representative democracy is not – at least rhetorically – the extent of Labour's democratic ambition, in or out of office. It is, however, typically the extent of what – in reality – it has offered in the past. In Chapter 4, I return to thinking about Labour's role in our democracy, based on its values.

The porters of Billingsgate fish market

The political scientist Peter Mair's brilliant *Ruling the Void*, published in 2013, told an important and influential story about contemporary European politics. What Hannah Arendt understood as the "public realm", the space where we discuss and act upon issues as political and social animals (Canovan 1995: 111), was being vacated by both citizens and political parties (Mair 2013: 16). Electorates identifying less and less with certain parties was mirrored by political parties identifying less and less with certain groups of voters (*ibid.*: 57). From a party political perspective, this saw a different kind of politics: one with less partisanship and a greater distance from citizens (*ibid.*: 82–3). One particular point stood out in Mair's thesis: parties had come "to think of themselves as self-sufficient and specialized political organizations, ready to heed cues from any of the range of social actors, but preferring to remain unrestricted by close formalized links with them" (*ibid.*: 85). Such a stance was epitomized by New Labour's rhetoric about the trade unions and an analysis of society that had moved beyond class (Evans & Tilley 2017). A political world (understood narrowly as "governing") and a social world (where the voters are) had become much more distinct (Mair 2013: 98). Mair summarized it very well indeed (*ibid.*: 98): "The result is the beginning of a new form of democracy, one in which the citizens stay at home while the parties get on with governing."

Motivated by a similar diagnosis, the Labour Party spent a great deal of time after New Labour – particularly after 2015 – attempting to change this. New Labour, the thinking went, had become the distant, professionalized, soulless political entity par excellence. "New Labour assumed the electorate would only respond to a sour, illiberal politics about consuming more, rather than deeper ideas of fraternity, of collective experience", the Labour MP Jon Cruddas wrote (2021: 151). In so doing, "New Labour lost its soul" (*ibid.*). In attempting to right this wrong, the last decade saw some well-known successes, including growing the Labour Party membership in a phenomenal way. Less well known is that, as with the story in Chapter 1, responding to the "void" was an immediate feature of the post-2010 political landscape, as people in the Labour Party sought to course-correct, moving away from New Labour and towards more participatory political practices.

The story starts with Blue Labour thinking, which gained prominence in 2010 during the battle of the Milibands and maintained influence through 2011 before petering out. Blue Labour, including the academic Maurice Glasman – made a life peer by Ed Miliband in 2011 – and other Labour actors, featured in the party's politics as an unstructured political moment rather than as an organized ideological faction. Cruddas, for example, was closely associated with the Blue Labour name but not defined by it. Rather than analysing a more programmatic, policy-based connection between Blue Labour and the Miliband leadership – which was often rhetorical but not substantive – the argument I make in this chapter is that Blue Labour thinking struck a chord with Labour people who felt, instinctively, that New Labour severed any meaningful connection between the party and communities, particularly working-class communities. The role of "organizing" within Blue Labour thinking was (and is, in Glasman's more recent restatement) of central importance: a rekindling of the politics of solidarity, institutions that buttress communities against the unforgiving power of capital and the meanings people take from that effort.

One such contribution in this vein came from Marc Stears, an academic and friend of Ed Miliband who would become Miliband's speechwriter up to the 2015 general election. In his contribution to a 2011 Blue Labour ebook – the product of seminars organized in the autumn of 2010 into the spring of 2011, which featured a preface from Miliband – Stears made the case for Labour to prioritize relationships and the "creation of a set of organizing structures and practices" that could help build solidarity from below (2011: 65). This required the party bringing people into political and social action where many may "have previously felt excluded". As Stears put it (*ibid.*: 66): "It is when people come together locally to save a library, help set up a new day care centre, or clean up decaying public spaces, that they begin to feel bonds of solidarity with each other that do not currently exist. This is a powerful basis for Labour renewal."

The party had to train community leaders and forget – or overcome – New Labour's suspicion of bottom-up community leadership (*ibid.*: 68). In words that would be echoed by the first national organizers of Momentum a few years later, Stears said Labour had "two key roles" to play. It must get election-ready "*and* it must be a force for immediate good in Britain today … building new possibilities where it can" (*ibid.*: 70, emphasis in original).

The training of community organizers was a feature of the 2010 Labour leadership contest from the beginning, with David Miliband announcing the creation of a "Movement for Change" to fund the training of 1,000 such organizers, something Ed Miliband later incorporated into his own vision for Labour's organizational change (Stratton 2011a). Part of this was undoubtedly motivated by "community organizing" becoming a political fashion. Barack Obama's 2007–8 presidential campaign was, of course, globally impactful. On the British left, Obama's rock star status was accompanied by a fascination with how his campaign had been organized, from small amounts of money being donated online to the commitment of organizers – a tradition of US community organizing, of which Obama himself had been a part – in helping to create an energizing momentum behind Obama's candidacy. Similar interest in the campaigning of US Senator Bernie Sanders, for the 2016 presidential nomination, was noticeable during the Corbyn years too.

But there were some internal Labour motivations as well. The consensus interpretation of New Labour (one broadly accepted by Blair) was that the project had failed to renew the party itself, or in Blair's words to build "a modern party base" (Blair 2011: x). In Ed Miliband's leadership launch article for *The Guardian*, he argued that Labour needed "to be not just an electoral force, but also a movement for change", the emblem of which was, for Miliband, a campaign for a living wage (2010a). How could Labour be turned into more than just a machine canvassing for votes? This is where Glasman entered the picture. Involved with London Citizens, part of Citizens UK – an organization working with community and religious groups to campaign for progressive change, including the London Living Wage campaign – Glasman engaged with both Milibands. He had an impact in terms of rhetoric: the language of "reciprocity" and "solidarity" in particular. However, there was little ideological or programmatic effect over the medium term, certainly in terms of headline policy. Coverage of Glasman's reported remarks on migration policy and Labour's record led to diminished influence (Bale 2015: 55), and while Glasman rowed back on how his remarks were presented (Wintour 2011b), they appeared to collide with the approach of many in and around the Labour Party. Rather, it was his initial pitch around Labour's organizational culture that had the greatest impact, speaking to the pitfalls of an overly technocratic and aloof political class. This was a critique the post-New Labour generation, including the Milibands, felt keenly.

In his later restatement of Blue Labour thinking, Glasman wrote that "a democratic self-governing society built upon the participation of its citizens in the exercise of power and its accountability is the fundamental goal of the Labour movement" (2022: 57). Redistribution by the state (through top-down tax and benefit changes, for example) is not rejected in this politics, but it is for the most part ignored; something which never spoke to Ed Miliband's political priorities and perhaps partly explains why Blue Labour also fell away quickly. Instead – and of real interest to Miliband at the time – Blue Labour featured a focus on community organizing and bottom-up institution building. "Organizing" meant "establishing relationships, not bringing people into an already agreed agenda": a "politics that is owned by local people" (*ibid.*: 111). It is a more literal understanding of the term "social democracy" (*ibid.*: 56) and finds expression in the creation of working-class and community institutions to resist the power of capital (*ibid.*: 58). In the early months after becoming Labour leader, Miliband visited one illustration of this that had caught Glasman's attention: the campaign of the porters of Billingsgate fish market in East London.

Along with Cruddas and Glasman, Miliband went to the early morning fish market in December 2010 (Stratton 2011b). He visited the café and heard from porters – workers moving the fish around the market site – about the City of London corporation, which manages the fish market, seeking to end "licences" for the porters working there (Boffey 2011). In other words, deregulating an aspect of the micro labour market at Billingsgate. The relevance for Glasman and Cruddas – and then to Miliband – was obvious. The status of the porters was an example of how rules and traditions represented what was both special about a job and a form of institutional power to resist the effects of globalization, deregulation and cheaper labour. Miliband told the Fabian Society the following month that his discussions at Billingsgate showed "why politicians should not shrug and walk away when they hear that traditional ways of life are under threat. We should seek to defend ways of life which give people self-respect" (Miliband 2011a). The asymmetry with New Labour was thought to be obvious here, with the "Third Way" response to this kind of issue likely to be around retraining and some redistribution as the global economy shifts the ground beneath people's feet. The purpose of the visit aimed to be distinctive too. Politicians meet people and visit places all the time; that isn't novel. Rather, the point here was that the organizing model was relational; in other words, this was a meeting to build a relationship (between a politician and the group of Billingsgate workers) and to lend support to a campaign, rather than receiving and adjudicating on demands in a more detached manner. The media did not attend.

There were big ambitions for this way of doing politics, at least at first. Miliband committed to changing Labour so that it was engaging with – and helping to drive – the campaigns of local organizations and groups around the country: bottom-up democratic practice and renewal. He argued (Miliband 2011a): "The only way we rebuild the case for politics is from the ground up. The campaign for the local library, the local zebra crossing, the improvement of a school, must be our campaign. And not just campaigns for the state to do things, but campaigns that achieve things in themselves."

Glasman put Miliband in touch with Arnie Graf, an experienced community organizer from the USA who had met with a young Obama to talk organizing (Merrick 2013). Graf got to work, with the enthusiastic backing of Miliband, seeking to understand how Labour engaged with communities and what it saw as a "campaign". He didn't recognize Labour "organizing" as organizing (Graf 2020: 191) but was soon engaged with Labour's regional staff to run an experiment: could Labour, in Lancashire, empower people's campaigns *and* benefit electorally in the process? This experiment included local Labour actors securing participation from Lancashire residents in devising manifesto policies, voting on them and campaigning. The emphasis was on relationships and securing commitment from those involved. Demands were bottom up, not top down. For Graf, it worked well, and people were reportedly positive about the results (*Ibid.*: 197–208). Yet it didn't last. By the time Labour's election strategy was coming together – to be headed up by the MP Douglas Alexander and the former Number 10 advisor Spencer Livermore – Graf didn't feel like he had the support of senior figures (*ibid.*: 211). According to Ed Miliband, Graf's "methods came up against the traditional ways of the Labour Party, and it's fair to say there was a clash of cultures with his ideas squeezed out by the demands of knocking on as many doors as possible" (Miliband 2021b: 214). "Organizing" was still a word heard often, but its meaning took on the more traditional Labour form of collecting data from electoral wards and asking people to vote Labour.

What of the story of Billingsgate? Miliband's politics of "One Nation", seen by commentators as a high point in his leadership, undoubtedly spoke to a feeling about New Labour and the politics of the 2000s: that it lacked connection and saw people as economic units rather than lives shaped by meaning as well as material circumstance. For Cruddas, "an over-reliance on distributional issues can appear indifferent to the wider emotional wellbeing of citizens and the lives they wish to live" (Cruddas 2021: 159), and this critique remained a part of Labour's politics. But any meaningful, deeper reflection on how the party operated ceased. Miliband did not appear to be comfortable with a more class-based politics, and his passion for campaigns such as the one for a living wage were as sources for ideas and manifesto commitments. The politics of the Billingsgate story are not uncomplicated either. On the one hand, the demands of the porters – particularly understood alongside Glasman's argument about globalization – were easy to comprehend and spoke to some of the problems of New Labour. A democratic deficit was also perceivable; without a different way of thinking about and conducting politics, who was listening to the porters' campaign? The licences for the porters were ended and claims were made about falling labour standards in the years that followed (Brown 2019).

Yet others argued the workplace culture needed to change, with the local MP at the time, Jim Fitzpatrick, suggesting that the market was "one of the last bastions of white male hegemony" (*ibid.*). The market is also soon to be on the move, joining another City of London market – the Smithfield meat market – at a new site in Dagenham. Billingsgate is currently nestled in the Docklands alongside some of the giants of global finance (the market is opposite Barclays, HSBC and KPMG at Canary Wharf). The market premises have an established but tired look. Is its move out of the Docklands an unforgiving but necessary change or an unjust one? Perhaps more importantly, the question of *who* decides that is a complicated one. Some people in and around the Labour Party would undoubtedly perceive a lack of justice, while being mindful of the dangers of nostalgia and of not seeing other, regressive power dynamics. Blue Labour thinking focused on the question of democracy and power as fundamental to Labour but too often ignored other political issues and values at stake. Core ideas about community organizing and empowering grassroots demands, however, did not go away. They came back with a bang in 2015.

Hegemonic bloc

In a scene symbolic of early "Corbynmania", Jeremy Corbyn addressed a crowd in a London street from the top of a fire engine, because of how oversubscribed one of his leadership campaign events was (Booth 2015). This kind of image became a familiar sight, but it also spoke to growing "movement politics", very literally. The fire engine in question was emblazoned "Fire Brigades Union" (FBU), and a little after Corbyn's leadership victory in September 2015, the FBU "reaffiliated" to the Labour Party, rejoining other trade unions as part of Labour's formal internal structures (FBU 2015). Trade union membership declined following Thatcherism and the economic changes of the 1980s. From a peak of over 13 million in Great Britain, the number of union members has roughly halved, standing at 6.67 million in 2019–20 (BEIS 2022: 6). As a proportion of employees, union membership has continued its decline, standing at fewer than a quarter of employees in the UK in 2021 (*ibid.*). Yet Labour's union–party link remained important during this time and survived what was seen by many as the hostility of some in New Labour. It did change though. As Webb and Bale noted, it came "to rest less on a sense of shared values and identity, and more on limited, instrumental exchanges of resources (from unions to party) and policy commitments (from party to unions)" (Webb & Bale 2017: 247). With Corbyn, the shared identity was back, and it was intrinsic to a project that wanted to bring organized labour, the Labour Party and social movements together.

The size of the Labour Party itself was also a feature of Corbyn's success and a product of movement politics from 2010 onwards. First, the 2015 leadership election took place under rules changed during Miliband's time as leader, where the so-called electoral college model for choosing a leader (one-third of votes for MPs, one-third for members, one-third for affiliates, e.g. trade union members) was abolished in favour of one person, one vote. Voters included the previous categories, with equal weight, plus a group of "registered supporters", who in 2015 could pay £3 for the right to vote in the leadership election. Registered supporters began under reforms devised by the Labour MP Peter Hain, in 2010, and were further developed after Miliband's changes to the leadership voting system, with the £3 fee decided later. While the idea of registered supporters spoke to Miliband's interest in movement politics, the changes to the leadership voting system were far more ad hoc (Bale 2015: 216–17; Kogan 2019: 191–200). Miliband had found himself under pressure to respond to allegations regarding union influence and "machine politics" in a parliamentary selection in Scotland (Miliband 2013a). By the time of Corbyn's election, registered supporters (since abolished under Starmer's leadership) had ballooned in number, with over 120,000 voting in the contest (Burton & Tunnicliffe 2022: 19).

Second, Labour's fee-paying membership experienced incredible growth following Corbyn's candidacy, in the face of much commentary on the decline of political parties. There was a modest rise in Labour's membership after the 2010 election, but under Corbyn the rise was huge, more than doubling in size to over half a million. Thanks to research about members of political parties, we also know more about who joined Labour and why. For example, we know that members who rejoined – having left under New Labour – were more left wing than existing or first-time members (Bale *et al.* 2020: 88). First-time members were more likely than rejoiners and existing members to feel "a degree of cynicism" about the way politics had been working (*ibid.*). And there is some evidence that, in the two years between 2015 and 2017 (Corbyn's first two years as leader), party members felt more listened to. When asked to consider the statement "the party leadership respects members", the percentage of members agreeing or strongly agreeing went from 69.6 per cent in 2015 to 91.1 per cent in 2017 (*ibid.*: 130). Overall, the movement was expanding, had new members and was enthusiastic about the prospect of a new politics. To make good on a lot of this, much hope was then invested in the new organization that had sprung from Corbyn's leadership campaign: Momentum.

Momentum – along with Corbyn project thinking on social movements more widely – was ambitious. Its first national organizers, including James Schneider, who would later become Corbyn's spokesperson, situated Momentum in the post-New Labour movement politics current, based on the Corbyn 2015 campaign (Klug *et al.* 2016: 38): "Corbyn put forward a new politics of bottom-up, participatory democracy, a new economics of shared prosperity, and a new relationship with the world based on solidarity and peace. These positions struck a chord with Labour members tired of top-down, neoliberal politics, and still angry about or ashamed by the Iraq War."

Momentum, they argued, comprised "post-financial crisis" social movements (such as Occupy), existing left protest movements (e.g. Stop the War) and the pre-existing Labour left, often still functioning around organizations from the Bennite era and the trade union left (*ibid.*: 37). Unsurprisingly keen for the enthusiasm generated around Corbyn's leadership campaign to be maintained, Momentum wanted to "build grassroots power" quickly, helping people organize "in their interests, through their own institutions" (*ibid.*: 36). For those concerned that this was a threat to the Labour Party (on the basis that it would distract from, or worse undermine, efforts to contact and communicate with "floating voters" in marginal seats), the organization's leaders stressed that such a move was not only in keeping with the party's past but not mutually exclusive from building a "campaigning machine" to win elections either. These were "dual aims" for the group (*ibid.*: 39). Overall, argued Momentum's organizers, the project wanted to "help organize a counter-hegemonic project of social blocs into a majority that can build a new social settlement" (*ibid.*; see also Schneider 2022: 46). This is political language in need of some explanation.

The dabbling with community organizing under Miliband's leadership was made more concrete during this period, and the political thinking around social movements more overtly theorized. From the outset there was an interest in political strategy and thinking influenced by the famous Italian political theorist Antonio Gramsci, an early twentieth-century communist imprisoned by Mussolini's fascist regime. The Marxist historian Eric Hobsbawm wrote in the mid-1990s that "such typically Gramscian terms as 'hegemony' occur in Marxist, and even in non-Marxist discussions of politics and history as casually, and sometimes as loosely, as Freudian terms did between the wars" (2012: 316). That trend returned during the Corbyn years, along with a connected and renewed interest in left populism (see Laclau 2018; Mouffe 2022). From Gramscian political thought came a cultural politics, one connected to a longstanding interpretation of Gramsci on the British left that pushed back at economic determinism (Maccaferri 2021). In other words, yes capital is powerful, but the ideology accompanying it should not be seen as irrelevant; rather, it contributes to the "hegemonic" nature of a liberal capitalist society. For that to be questioned required a battle in this cultural and political territory associated with the term "war of position" (*ibid.*), seeking to achieve a new common sense. This kind of thinking partly underpinned those early statements from Momentum, alongside a particular understanding of "populism".

Left populism built on some of Gramsci's theory. Often associated with the political theorists Ernesto Laclau and Chantal Mouffe, populism was described by Laclau as a "political logic" (2018: 117). In the context of heterogeneous demands, populist logic foresees the division of society into two parts and the articulation of a "people" around what Laclau called "equivalential relations" (*ibid.*: 93). The key part of this "logic" is the transcending of heterogeneous demands to the point of one collective identity, "the people" (*ibid.*). In more recent work thinking through this left populist logic, Mouffe has argued for a politics geared around climate change as well as economic antagonisms (2022: 62). The "left" part of the description, and the fact that what left populist theorists articulate is not an ideology per se, is important for distinguishing between this "kind" of populism and – for example – populist radical right politicians. The latter are not pluralist, the former can be pluralist; "the people" is understood in left populism as a way of bringing diverse demands together, not articulating a homogenous identity of "a people" who should hold the political power (Moffitt 2020: 26–7). One thing the different kinds of populism arguably do share, in practice, is an aspect discussed by Moffitt in a discussion of populism and democracy: the potential for leaders to take on a claim to "infallibility and unchallengeability" (*ibid.*: 110; see also Bolton & Pitts 2018: 61).

Much of this can feel far away from the day-to-day Labour Party and its role in our democracy. Some of the language is inaccessible, which is perhaps unfortunate when the thinking is not too dissimilar to coalition-building, albeit with more of a focus on movement politics. What's important for us here is that people coming to Labour, and engaging with the debates about what the party should do after New Labour, were curious about the role of social movements and open to rethinking how a political party should operate. They were conscious too of wider European and global currents on the left engaged with some of the same thinking, for instance Podemos in Spain (Errejón & Mouffe 2016). All of this required navigating what is often seen as a boundary between two very different things: social movements articulating specific demands and working towards cultural change, and political parties adjudicating upon demands, and those of others, in the context of political values (see Avril 2019: 256–8). On the left of politics, where many social movements often seem to have overlapping values with parties – for example, tackling poverty and inequalities of power and wealth – there is an obvious and open question as to whether the two can complement one another, particularly when a political party is out of power and campaigning for change.

During the Corbyn period, observers asked whether a dialectical process was possible, where social movements saw more clearly the partisan nature of issues and a less professionalized and managerial class let go of some political control (White & Ypi 2016: 29). Others pointed to an ongoing conceptual confusion, with the language of social movements and movement building being misapplied or misunderstood (Thompson 2016). For some on the left, the Corbyn project could only succeed if traditional electoral politics not only became less professionalized but to a great extent got out of the way. Left activists and thinkers saw great potential in Corbynism but noted the differences between a political party they traditionally invested little hope in (and which Corbyn now led) and the promise of social movements. Hilary Wainwright, a longstanding contributor to debates on the British left, argued that the Corbyn project's "prospects turn on whether he can reverse the traditional logic of electoral politics, whereby the people cede their power to their political representatives. Corbyn's 'new politics' is about political representatives using the platform of the state to empower popular forces" (2016).

For the academic Keir Milburn, who put forward the thesis of a "left generation" following the experience of the global financial crisis, movement politics was essential to changing the country's political culture, creating space for a project such as Corbyn's and exercising "extra-parliamentary forms of power" against capital (2019: 100). There was a substantive clash, though, between movement politics and political parties, with electoral politics producing "its own temporality of electoral cycles which don't fit the temporality of movements" (*ibid.*: 101). Meanwhile, how workable was a populist approach, understood as "a cohesion of diverse demands and struggles into a single political antagonism" (Schneider 2022: 58), in what was becoming a UK polity pulling itself apart? Would an anti-austerity message change the conversation in Scotland, with a dominant SNP and a nation divided on the subject of independence? And after the Brexit shock in 2016 gave way to a time-limited period of the status quo for Britain and Europe, could such an antagonism be held together?

Elections, elections, elections

Corbyn's period as Labour leader was often frantic, jostled from crisis to confidence and back again by a number of very consequential electoral moments: from Corbyn's understated performance in the EU referendum, to the relative jubilation of the 2017 election and the misery of 2019. That electoral record is the subject of immense factional mythologizing within Labour. For Corbyn supporters, 2017 is the event of record, and showed that Corbyn's politics could change the electoral arithmetic and challenge conventional wisdom. For those critical of Corbyn's leadership, the Brexit referendum and the 2019 election are the events of record, showing that Corbynism was a disaster, upholding the conventional wisdom. For this chapter, the relevance of the (many) elections Corbyn experienced as leader is to divide our story of movement politics into a tale of two elections: 2017 and 2019. Labour "won the ground war" in 2017 (Cowley & Kavanagh 2018: 436), and the shock result played its part in maintaining support (for a while) for movement politics. The 2019 contest exposed the fragile underpinnings of this movement politics and shattered the Corbyn project.

At Labour's annual conference in 2016, supporters of the Corbyn project launched and ran "The World Transformed" (TWT), which operated alongside the conference. Inside a Liverpool venue, the idea of a political project sustained by and embracing social movements was palpable. Flags and emblems of social movements were displayed around a central room, with unions, climate activism and campaigns set up to protest acts of state violence. TWT in 2016 included events that were different to typical conference fringe gatherings: usually panel events with politicians, journalists and representatives of non-governmental organizations, trade unions, employer associations or private companies. TWT was activist-focused and provided a platform for those who constituted movement politics, including organizations that provided political education and organizing support. It was a manifestation of the kinds of groups the Corbyn project believed were key to the cultural politics they wanted to run.

With hindsight, while Labour continued to struggle in the polls, and Theresa May wrestled with the high politics of preparing for Brexit negotiations and her vision of a new meritocracy, this first TWT was the beginning of a confident period for Corbynism, albeit a short-lived one. John McDonnell has since reflected on the motivations behind this kind of politics, noting (2021, 146) that social movements are about not "just bodies who go out knocking on doors, but creating an engaged, active participation". "It's the Gramscian concept of hegemony. You create a climate of opinion where everything you're doing, people can just say, well, that's common sense ... [If Corbyns' Labour had succeeded] we would have built up the social movement in such a way that we won every argument."

If this sounds like an incredibly optimistic statement from McDonnell, that's because it is: an optimism bound up with a belief in movement politics as the key to political success, particularly for a left political project subject to constant criticism. But while the outward manifestation of a social movement was there for all to see at Labour's 2016 conference, and the 2017 general election – followed by the "Oh Jeremy Corbyn" euphoria at Glastonbury and beyond – was evidence for Corbyn's team of the success of an anti-austerity movement (Schneider 2022: 12), some Corbyn supporters have since noted the beginning of the end for this attempt at movement politics.

Michael Chessum worked with Momentum and Corbyn's team before leading an anti-Brexit campaign that brought his activism into conflict with the very project that had seemed to be *the* political vehicle for the post-financial crisis social movements referred to above (Chessum 2022: 62). Yet, as I noted when introducing the ambitious beginnings of Momentum, that left generation was not the only element constituting the Corbyn project, and therefore not the only guide as to the path it could take. For Chessum, the key problem for Corbynism was that people could not agree on how to channel the political energy created between 2015 and 2017. Indeed, "for many of its key protagonists [the pre-existing Labour left within Corbynism], its crucial promise was not about social movements or a new mass politics but about winning elections inside Labour and changing the party's structures" (Chessum 2022: 133). In short, factionalism. This was evidenced early on in Momentum's development, with the figure of Jon Lansman, a Bennite veteran of the Labour left and long-time organizer with the Campaign for Labour Party Democracy, seen as emblematic of the internal Labour tendency (*ibid.*: 138).

Corbyn has since reflected on his project's attempts at movement building, although in a narrower way than McDonnell and those who worked with him at the time. He noted something many people in and around Labour would agree with: that local Labour Party meetings can be quite boring and unwelcoming. Yet on building a movement, his reasoned critique focused on the failure to establish a community organizing team quickly, referencing the kind of opposition Graf talked about during the Miliband years:

[I] wanted the party to be a much more democratic and responsible organization, with a community presence all over the country. The Labour Party cannot win in the long run if all it does is play a media game and pursue a Westminster strategy. It has to be a real presence in the community in order to mobilize people ... The greatest resistance I had within the party bureaucracy and structures was to the establishment of community organizing. They wanted to continue in the old way. (Corbyn 2020).

For some Corbyn sceptics in the party at the time, the community organizing team was suspected of being a factional entity for internal organizing as well as for outward-facing work. Zarah Sultana, the Labour MP in Coventry South who was previously an organizer, argued after the team was scrapped under Starmer's leadership that "admiration for community organizing is hardly a factional trait" (2021). Rightly noting that the Miliband brothers had shown a keen interest, Sultana put the case that Labour could only achieve lasting change "by building grassroots power, bringing working class people together" (*ibid.*). It's on this point where some on the left have pointed to a weakness in Corbyn's plan. More sympathetically, Schneider noted that the regular electoral cycles meant the unit was focused on those contests "rather than deep organizing" (2022: 50). More critically, Chessum argued that the approach to community organizing was top down, while empowering the activists already there (e.g. people having joined Momentum) was a more obviously grassroots approach (2022: 158). Indeed, going much further in his criticism, Chessum suggested that having "defined themselves in opposition to New Labour's managerial style", the Corbyn project ended up in a similar place, viewing "much of its own activist base with suspicion" (*ibid.*: 172).

After 2017, the British political debate was transformed by a looming Brexit deadline, a Conservative Party with an increasingly Eurosceptic wing and a Labour Party torn between voters in Leave-supporting seats and its overwhelmingly pro-European membership. The context presented a democratic dilemma: if the opinions of Labour's members were indicative of the beliefs and aspirations of the movement that had sprung up around Corbynism in 2015, then the party had to take heed of those demands and, as a movement, achieve the softest Brexit, or preferably prevent it from happening at all. The campaigns that sought to achieve the latter became very high profile. Yet there was an ideological and electoral flipside. Some of those within the Corbyn project, long agnostic or antagonistic towards the EU, saw little of merit to fight for. To support a pro-Brexit position, they could point to Labour seats that supported Leave and the threat to democracy from ignoring them, further pushing Labour voters (and working-class voters) away from an out-of-touch political party, the very opposite of what Corbynism could achieve.

Some of the subsequent analysis of this period has a factional lean. Oliver Eagleton, in his critical biography of Keir Starmer, argued that "given the degree of enthusiasm for Corbyn's leadership among rank-and-file Labour activists, LOTO [the leader's office] knew it could secure the membership's support for … [a] progressive Leave policy, even if the majority of them had voted Remain in 2016" (2022: 86). This is a heroic claim. Asked in 2017 whether there should be a referendum on a final deal, 81.9 per cent of Labour members agreed. More than 90 per cent backed staying in the single market and customs union (Bale *et al.* 2020: 66). By 2018, Theresa May had a Brexit deal, but the political outlook was gloomy for the then prime minister. When asked again, Labour members backed a referendum on the deal by a similar margin: 88 per cent said they'd vote remain (assuming that was an option) in a referendum. When asked to weight positive feelings about different outcomes, the UK having a new referendum and voting to remain was the highlight, some distance ahead of leaving but staying in the single market and customs union (*ibid.*: 68). To suggest there wasn't a clash between a Labour Party that was against Brexit and a Leave-supporting ideology (backed by serious electoral concern) is simply not the case. Labour's 2017 conference witnessed accusations of limiting debate on Brexit, with no specific votes on single market membership, for example (Walker *et al.* 2017).

In 2018, with the People's Vote and the Another Europe is Possible anti-Brexit campaigns gaining influence, Len McCluskey, the head of the Unite union, warned that any prospective referendum should not have Remain as an option (Walker *et al.* 2018). A conference motion committing the party to backing a referendum on a Brexit deal – if a general election couldn't be forced instead – was passed, although there was still rancour. Keir Starmer made an intervention with his speech to the conference, saying Remain was not being ruled out as an option. McCluskey's deputy followed it up by contradicting Starmer (Stewart & O'Carroll 2018). The following year, with an election against Boris Johnson's Conservatives highly likely, debate continued. The party's position was ultimately that a Corbyn government would seek to negotiate a new Brexit deal, have a referendum and offer people the choice of taking the new deal or remaining. The party's official line on the preferred choice was ambiguous, to be decided later. It was the messy compromise of party management, with Momentum and the trade unions acting to support Corbyn's leadership, seeking to prevent what they saw as further undermining of his authority.

Brexit marked the end of the Corbyn project's ambitions for movement politics, but that isn't the whole story about the flawed process of building a movement during this period. Two separate points must be made. The first is about factionalism. For the Labour Party to be more democratic, it has to be a movement that is accepting of dissent (Creasy & Pike 2021: 44). That was not the case during the Corbyn years, where longstanding Labour actors witnessed party meetings become "a bad-tempered battleground of procedural conflict" (Harman 2017: 352). No doubt the context is relevant. Factionalism is a contingent thing, based in part on long-established rivalries and competing histories, as well as power relations within a political party. Corbyn's leadership was criticized a great deal, and the leadership felt under attack from internal doubters. Yet, as Chessum noted, not only was Corbynism, as a movement, directed towards factional gain, but "as far as many were concerned, you could either defend Jeremy or betray him" (2022: 191). Factionalism is constituted in part by political differences, but factionalism also entrenches and enhances those differences, leading to the creation of enemies rather than political sparring partners. No doubt Corbyn's backers often felt angry at the lack of support from Labour's MPs; indeed part of their strategy for political survival was to confront the parliamentary party with a wider movement (Watts & Bale 2019: 105–8). Regardless, it was not an environment conducive to the politics that Labour's members had been promised.

The second point is Corbyn's greatest failure of leadership: Labour's antisemitism crisis. This caused suffering to Jewish people inside and outside of the Labour Party. Labour politicians were targeted with abuse for being Jewish and for raising concerns about antisemitism within the Labour Party. People protested in Parliament Square, holding "Enough is Enough" signs and asking for far greater action to prevent antisemitism within Labour. Luciana Berger left Labour because of how the party responded to the concerns, noting that the toll of it all "made me physically ill" (Kentish 2019). She has since rejoined the party, following Starmer's response in tackling antisemitism since becoming leader. When Corbyn responded to questions about antisemitism within the Labour Party, he did so – and has since – in an often exasperated manner, when many rightly expected (and still today expect) a sense of profound sorrow.

The Equality and Human Rights Commission (EHRC) published a damning report in 2020, and "concluded that there were unlawful acts of harassment and discrimination for which the Labour Party is responsible" (2020: 6). The report noted that "it is hard not to conclude that antisemitism within the Labour Party could have been tackled more effectively if the leadership had chosen to do so" (*ibid.*: 6). It documented examples of Labour members sharing antisemitic content online. Overall, the EHRC noted (*ibid.*: 101): "We find that the Labour Party has failed to address antisemitism within the party in a way that demonstrates its stated commitment to zero tolerance, or that ensures all Jewish members feel welcome and can be confident that antisemitism will be dealt with effectively."

Corbyn had the Labour whip suspended in the House of Commons, owing to his response to the publication of the EHRC report. He was prevented from standing as a future Labour candidate by the National Executive Committee. It is to Keir Starmer's credit that the EHRC has since concluded that Labour has made the necessary changes to its procedures (EHRC 2023), something he rightly prioritized when taking over the leadership.

The democratic deficit

"The Westminster system is part of the problem", Starmer declared in a 2023 New Year's speech. Buoyed by positive opinion polling for Labour, a more confident Starmer set out a compelling critique of a political system that hoards power in Westminster and Whitehall and too often runs from one issue to another, driven in part by the media. He argued (Starmer 2023a): "sometimes I hear talk about a 'huge day in Westminster', but all that's happened is someone has passionately described a problem ... Nothing has changed, but the circus moves on ... I call it 'sticking plaster politics'".

Starmer's response to this problem was two-pronged. To guide central government in taking the big strategic decisions, Labour announced a set of national missions (discussed in Chapter 1). To end the centralization in Westminster and Whitehall, Labour committed to devolving power. Gordon Brown led a commission examining the latter on Starmer's behalf, deploying the mantra of "ensuring the right powers are in the right places" (Labour Party 2022c: 8). The starting point, the commission's final report argued, had to be a "system of decision making that does not start from the top – but starts from the people and is grounded in new ways of consulting, participating, and deciding" (*ibid.*: 8). The right power in the right places did not necessarily mean one level down from central government, for example from Whitehall to a local authority or agency. "Double devolution", devolving power further down, from local authorities to community groups, for example, was possible too. Such thinking reminds us of a recurring dilemma that has featured in this chapter: that posed by relinquishing control while ensuring Labour's values are put into action. The response of Labour's commission was to partner decentralization with individual rights, such as people always having access to universal healthcare (*ibid.*: 12).

Labour's report added up to ambitious constitutional change. Other suggestions included the drafting of a statement of the UK's social and economic ambitions, such as the eradication of poverty. This too would involve citizen participation in its formulation, through citizens' assemblies (*ibid.*: 144). There was also the headline-grabbing proposal to replace the House of Lords with a democratic Assembly of the Nations and Regions (something, in one form or another, Labour has committed to before), and much more on devolving power to the Scottish parliament (*ibid.*: 9–10). Overall, the focus was on distributing power, and a process of democratizing the state and its decision-making. Labour, following a tradition prominent in the story of this chapter, is today seeking a more participatory approach to Britain's democracy, addressing Mair's "void" through reform of the state. Politics would move closer to the people, and citizens (it is expected) would move closer to politics, participating through deliberation but also in decision-making and delivery.

A driving force behind these ideas for Labour has been the MP for Wigan, Lisa Nandy, who has consistently argued that a disconnect exists between the preoccupations of Westminster (and London and the south-east) and those of much of the rest of the country. Intellectually curious and sceptical of factionalism, Nandy often embraced the complexity of both democratic processes and policymaking after being elected in 2010. In the aftermath of the Brexit referendum, Nandy adopted an approach that at least left the door open to working with the then Conservative prime minister, Theresa May. For Nandy, Labour's posture on Brexit had to recognize and respond to a growing distance between the party and the people. Opposing it had, she argued, "played into the sense that we are adrift from communities like these [Wigan], that we don't speak for them, we don't stand for them, we don't understand them, and worse than that: we're deeply disrespectful towards them. And that has been building for the last 15 to 20 years" (Mason 2019). Having been a candidate in the 2020 Labour leadership contest, coming third out of the three, Nandy joined Starmer's shadow cabinet, first shadowing the Foreign Office, then moving to responsibility for "levelling up", before returning to the Foreign Office team in a less senior role. Nandy's politics, and her advocacy within Labour, were much affected by an interpretation of New Labour.

If socialism is, fundamentally, about changing social relationships to bring about a more equal society, New Labour, for Nandy, forgot about the people – the "social" – meaning the party "lost" a tradition to "the paternalism and technocratic approach that came to characterize our recent past ... Sharing power was once a core part of our history. It is central to our future" (Nandy 2022: 127).

As with the prevailing narrative since 2010 about New Labour, power and the people, Nandy's thesis was similar to the zeitgeist Peter Mair elaborated on in *Ruling the Void*. "While people can rail against the system," Nandy wrote, "they cannot change it. It is a democratic deficit" (2022: 107). Her ideas included moves towards a more participatory democratic system, including in policy development and political prioritization (*ibid*.: 127, 164). This is one of the democratic threads running through the post-New Labour years, partly based on an interpretation of New Labour that saw the party as accepting the norms of globalization and adopting policies that would lead to strong growth and more opportunity in only some places. Indeed, according to Nandy, New Labour went further than acceptance: it moved to "embrace" globalization (Nandy 2023: 16). Investment in infrastructure and redistribution formed the response to those deemed to have "lost" something to the globalized economy (*ibid*.: 17). For

Nandy and others – including those associated with Blue Labour, considered earlier in this chapter – New Labour's approach led to a democratic divorce with communities across the country, particularly in the north of England. Following this interpretation, redistribution is necessary but not sufficient: people need more power over their economic and social environment.

Labour's commitment to devolution predates Starmer's leadership. Gordon Brown showed a particular interest in different forms of civic engagement (citizens' "juries", as they were then called), and devolution was a part of Miliband's agenda. Yet – and this was the case with Brown and Miliband, owing in large part to the global financial crisis – the political context is not always conducive to the prioritization of political reform. With Starmer, the prioritization of it has been backed up by substantive policy thinking, rhetorical strategies and a connection to Starmer's political purpose: one of the selling points of his leadership has been his presentation as someone keen to get things done, building a narrative on the basis of his past experience, including as director for public prosecutions. The easy politics of criticizing Westminster is there but repackaged, not as decrying a political elite but targeting an overcentralized system where the wrong people are taking the decisions. Of course, none of this is uncomplicated. Redistributing decision-making power is one thing, giving people the resources to realize different choices and decisions is another. Likewise the optimism of thinking that more local layers of politics will always deliver things better: they may do, but they may also experience their share of mismanagement and poor judgement.

The more pressing point for this chapter is an apparent absence for Starmer: the role of movement politics, and of community organizing, as part of the Labour Party's democratic practice. In seeking to devolve decision-making power, and to democratize much of public policy, the role of both movements and organizing is notably missing from Labour's current thinking. Social movements have achieved significant impacts in the first quarter of the twenty-first century, even if the central government response has too often been found wanting. What political scientists think of as power over the political agenda (Lukes 2021: 30) is democratized in part by powerful social movements: in other words, movements that are already achieving change by shifting the conversation from the grassroots and demanding a response. If Labour's political plan involves a different, more responsive political system, then the importance of movements and grassroots campaigns to the party's politics is undeniable.

Starmer's own response to the power of contemporary social movements has been disjointed. The Labour leader expressed regret for his use of the word "moment" to describe the Black Lives Matter movement (BBC News 2020), later telling a journalist from *The Voice* (2020) that "[w]hat I meant by a 'moment' was a 'defining moment', or a 'turning point'. If I've heard anything in the last few weeks and months, that has been loud and strong and clear, is that the BLM [Black Lives Matter] movement, and the emotional coming together that's happened in the last few weeks and months has to be a turning point."

In his 2021 conference speech, Starmer sought to defend the England men's football team, who had taken the knee prior to their matches in the European Championship of that year, arguing that showing patriotism was to support the players in doing so. Labour trod a fine line on the Conservative government's legislative efforts to highlight "culture war" issues, including limits to protest and custodial sentences for damaging statues – the party opposed this legislation while noting its support for the police and the criminal justice system. A resurgent trade union movement, leading strikes over pay and conditions during a cost-of-living crisis, similarly saw Labour adopt a circumspect political strategy. On the one hand, the party has been clear in its opposition to Conservative measures to limit the right to strike. On the other hand, Starmer has been equally clear that he seeks a distance between Labour and unions leading strikes, and I return to this topic in Chapter 3. Mick Lynch, the leader of the RMT union, described the industrial action as an example of a wider movement politics that Starmer is reluctant to join. "The trade unions are reinvigorating themselves," he argued, "but we now need the political side, the cultural side, and all the rest of it to follow suit." While acknowledging that Labour's political programme was the party's responsibility, Lynch suggested that "Keir Starmer and the leadership will have to show that they identify with this growing movement" (Lynch 2022: 11).

The essential point from all of this is that if Labour is serious about efforts *in government* to further democratize politics and to empower local communities to make decisions, then Labour *as a political party* needs to adopt a different attitude to power and political control too. A more participatory democratic model requires more civic engagement, political education and organization at the grassroots: all features of social movements and campaign groups, from the local to the national and international. To be responsive to local campaigns, and to lead campaigns locally, means reflecting once again on the practices of community organizing discussed earlier. If Labour is running a local authority, and has succeeded in devolving so much power, then the party will need to change to provide a system of accountability for itself. It will need to be open to community groups, to criticism and to people who are invested in local political change as much as at the national level. If Labour is not running a local authority, its style of politics needs to undergo a similar change, with much more of its day-to-day campaigning done through the lens of local campaign groups, rather than top-down politics. Lisa Nandy has been very alive to this challenge, noting that throughout the country "you will find Labour Party members organizing … volunteering in community centres. They'll be running the local foodbank … they're doing it as community activists. I think what this means for the Labour

Party is that will become far more visible ... a far more obvious part of our approach" (Nandy 2023: 22).

This change is important for avoiding the replication of political representation that seems distant from communities, even if the level of governance has shifted. The risk, as Sartori put it, is "the displacement by counter-elites of pre-existing elites" (1987: 116).

In February 2023, journalists at *Politico* noted that Starmer had "been less squeamish about talking directly to Blair about policy and strategy ideas, as well as to Blair's immediate successor as PM, Gordon Brown" (Dickson & Webber 2023). As I suggested in the introduction to this book, part of the attraction for Starmer in speaking with Blair and Brown stems from his focus on winning elections. For Starmer, the reaction to New Labour over the last decade has been at least partly problematic in Labour forgetting how to win. On movement politics, however, Blair's thinking appears out of step with the political times and the changes planned by Labour, including those suggested by Gordon Brown. In an interview about winning back "Red Wall" constituencies following Labour's 2019 electoral collapse, Blair suggested that "whether it's Black Lives Matter, Extinction Rebellion, MeToo, trans rights, if you look as if you're in a negotiation with those groups over policy, you're not going to get those people [Red Wall voters] back" (Payne 2021: 124). The possible inferences from Blair, here, are many, as are the contradictions. One important point for the argument of this chapter is that, when letting go of some political control, and adopting a more bottom-up approach to politics and democracy, the participation of people, movements and communities is part of the process. Politics has, perhaps, started to move on. Labour should be a part of that.

Conclusion

This chapter has shown how interpretations of New Labour motivated a shift towards movement politics after 2010, from Miliband's fleeting interest in community organizing to the Corbyn project's ambitions for a social movement and the early promises from those involved in Momentum. A decade of electoral failure has diminished the significance of this thinking, and its promise was never realized. Yet both the motivations for, and insights from, movement politics have not gone away. Nor were they solely a UK phenomenon; rather, "a combination of citizen disaffection with representative politics and a global democratic 'push' have led parties in all liberal democracies to design new ways to connect with their electorates and to seek inspiration from other organizing models" (Avril 2019: 259).

During Starmer's leadership, Labour's response to concern about a democratic deficit has focused on devolving decision-making power away from Westminster, building on the approach of Brown, Miliband and Corbyn before him. Starmer's antipathy towards the Westminster system appears genuine and is often convincing, contributing to his diagnosis of a wider British political malaise: must everything, he has asked, be so dysfunctional? With input from other influential Labour figures, the party's proposals for devolving power now form a significant part of its political programme. Yet movement politics is noticeably absent from this discourse. Labour continues to tread carefully in its response to social movements, seeking to maintain control of the party's image and its messaging. Yet decentralizing decision-making and engaging with campaign groups are two things that should not be allowed to diverge. On the contrary, aligning the policy and the practice is critical to the success of the former. There is no single, successful blueprint from the past decade for how Labour can make a more democratic politics work. However, if Labour is today committed to trusting people and relinquishing decision-making power from Westminster, it needs to keep trying. That's what the telic understanding of democracy tells us.

If Labour is to succeed in a decentralized and democratized political landscape, the party needs to change too. There are elements of movement logic and thinking – in particular, that of community organizing and empowering communities to decide their own priorities – that came to life in response to New Labour's legacy and remain relevant. There is of course much to disagree about in political debates on the left, but this chapter has shown how concerns about democracy, and how to enliven it, have been shared across different political traditions. As the labour movement began to achieve greater prominence during the cost-of-living crisis, Mick Lynch argued that democracy had "decayed" in Britain. "We have left it to a professional class", he suggested, "and that has been to our detriment" (Lynch 2022: 10). This is the political thread connecting the many different voices considered in this chapter, and has formed a shared interpretation and response to the politics of New Labour and the wider politics of the beginning of the twenty-first century. The term "extra-parliamentary" has often been used to describe movement politics, as an alternative to parliamentary politics throughout Labour's history (Gamble 2021: 174–5). Part of the promise of Starmer's political programme – albeit one relatively unremarked upon – is to decentralize British politics in a way that moves beyond Westminster and so ends that particular dichotomy.

3
POLITICS: HEAD AND HEART

Introduction

The Welsh actor Michael Sheen is not only well known for his film and television drama roles but also his stirring rhetoric on and off screen. Before a motivational speech for the Wales men's football team in 2022 was widely shared, Sheen had gone viral before: with a speech about Aneurin Bevan and the NHS, on St David's Day, prior to the 2015 general election. On Bevan, Sheen told a watching crowd that the politician who had founded the NHS "didn't care what the polls were saying" (Sheen 2015). Instead, "this was a man who had no fear in standing up for what he believed in". To contemporary politicians, who Sheen described as "scared of saying what they feel for fear of alienating a part of the electorate ... too careful to speak from their hearts", the actor warned (*ibid.*): "There is never an excuse to not speak up for what you think is right. You must stand up for what you believe. But first of all – by God, believe in something." In his speech, Sheen posited a form of political judgement and style that will be recognizable, both from other advocates and from critics: you *must* speak from principle, even with fear of an electoral cost. With Bevan as his subject, Sheen's speech also invoked Labour's radical, working-class identity and its postwar glory years: a time, in this retelling, of politicians unafraid to paint in primary colours. This meeting point for different meanings – moral, ethical, emotional and historical – gives rise to the different kinds of politics that are the focus of this chapter.

Those in and around the Labour Party have heard many politicians empathize about a problematic policy, or acknowledge the unfairness of something, yet prevaricate on the way forward. Critics of New Labour have remarked upon "its perceived triangulation and spinning" (Jones 2020: 52), the substitution of ambiguity for core values or worse a wholesale embrace of neoliberal politics. The certainty with which the latter interpretation is often expressed is not supported by the evidence (Wickham-Jones 2021), yet towards the end of New Labour's time in office, in lieu of a clear expression of belief was a mixture of viewpoints, derived from opinion polling and repeated back at the electorate.

It was no longer a coherent project, a point made by people in and around the Labour Party and featured in Chapter 1. A focus on spin, and criticism of vacuity, led to a boon for satirists (e.g. *The Thick of It*). When running for the Labour leadership, Ed Miliband seized upon and attacked the suggestion that being unapologetic about Labour's values was a hostage to fortune. He saw it as a part of the New Labour playbook that needed to be torn out and binned. However, one Corbyn-supporting commentator saw a version of New Labour's triangulation persisting under Miliband's leadership. Evoking the image of a zombie political strategy, Seymour claimed that "New Labour was not dead; it was undead" (2016: 178). The Corbyn project's raison d'être was speaking and acting on the basis of principle (*ibid.*: 23), putting this particular zombie out of its misery and embracing meanings that New Labour had sought to bury, including class politics (Pidcock 2019). Yet, once again, the ambitions of the Corbyn project were not fulfilled. On Brexit, Corbyn triangulated, seeking to avoid taking sides, with his reputation for speaking from principle "obliterated" (Jones 2020: 5). Partly motivated by fears of losing some Labour heartlands that had backed Leave, Labour adopted numerous (and often unclear) Brexit positions, losing working-class voters anyway. Corbyn ended his tenure as a symbol of a politics others fought over.

Keir Starmer has gotten quite used to people criticizing him for being boring. Unlike Miliband, and Corbyn, he is unabashed in his preference for technocracy over "shouting on a soap box" (Wearmouth 2022). "People often say: where is the passion?" he told one journalist (*ibid.*). "The passion is in fixing the problems. What I don't like is people who speak passionately about a problem over and over again, as they walk around it." This is a different Starmer from the one promising to "make the moral case for socialism" after Labour's 2019 defeat (Starmer 2020) and marks a different style to that of Miliband and Corbyn. Of course, "fixing" things and adopting a values-led approach to a more ethical society are not mutually exclusive. The question within Labour's politics is about how the party's politicians arrive at everyday political and moral judgements, in the context of an often sceptical electorate and a critical media reluctant to report on nuance, and operating in the reactive environment of opposition. Many of these decisions can be accompanied by a "moral cost" (Williams 1981: 63), a key idea in this chapter which I explain below. In Starmer's argument above, we get a glimpse of the thinking that is often involved in such judgements. For Starmer, there is little to be gained from the rhetoric of protest: the inference of "soap box" language. Any moral cost from not protesting is dwarfed by a much bigger one: Labour being out of power and unable to fix things.

As I noted in the Introduction, the dichotomies that Labour's actors use in thinking through how to conduct politics – for example, power versus protest – tell us something about different political identities within the Labour Party.

People on the left demonstrate broad "expressive" and "instrumental" orientations to varying extents (Parkin 1968: 34). Yet while such sociological categorization is useful, at the root of these characterizations are the different beliefs and feelings involved in making choices (Midgley 1983: 86). Utilizing the work of Bernard Williams, I show in this chapter how what he termed a "sensibility to moral costs" (1981: 63) is an essential insight into understanding how some people sought to move on from New Labour, and to find what they believed to be a better balance of the party's values and the electoral imperative. The New Labour approach was associated with what I term a "utilitarian presumption" – derived from Williams' interpretation and critique of utilitarianism (Smart & Williams 1973) – that said if the preferences of Labour's decision-makers appeared out of step with public opinion, symbolic moments to correct that perception needed to be seized upon.

These moments sometimes involved choices that witnessed a clash between Labour values and the perceived electoral need. Critically, the utilitarian approach does not recognize a moral cost in such a clash, for the (hoped for) outcome would be a better chance of Labour winning or continuing in power: a greater good. Here, the thinking is related to an interpretation of utilitarianism that "requires simply *adding up* individual welfares or utilities to assess the consequences" (Sen and Williams 1982: 4). Tough decisions to back policies or deploy rhetoric that resulted in a clash could be taken, then, for a greater good. The utilitarian presumption is, I argue, dominant in Starmer's worldview, making him a different leader to his post-2010 predecessors. Yet Starmer's self-confessed ruthlessness is only sometimes partnered with conviction. Alongside a sense of being rudderless, ruthlessness can be a negative force, leading to inconsistency. I begin the chapter with some examples of what I mean by everyday moral judgements, the first of which is an intervention from Tony Blair after he left office.

Resisting the temptation

In April 2013, with Ed Miliband a third of the way through his third full year as Labour leader, Tony Blair took to the pages of the *New Statesman*, a leading magazine for the Labour commentariat. As I showed in Chapter 1, Miliband ended up equivocating between a focus on an unequal, broken economic system and addressing Labour's post-financial crisis legacy. From the left, his approach was branded "austerity-lite". In other words, he would follow the Conservative Party's approach, albeit in a less damaging form. From the Labour right, Miliband was accused of being insufficiently "in touch" and "centrist" on welfare, while failing to defend Labour's record prior to the crash. In the April of 2013, Conservative Chancellor George Osborne was under increasing pressure over his austerity cuts and poor UK economic performance (Elliot 2013). Yet Blair was uncomfortable with Labour's strategic direction, not because the Conservative plan was fair and just, but because Labour's approach threatened its chances of taking office. Labour, Blair wrote, was "back as the party opposing 'Tory cuts', highlighting the cruel consequences" being felt by people. Yet this situation was "more menacing" than it appeared. He wrote (Blair 2013):

> The ease with which it [Labour] can settle back into its old territory of defending the status quo, allying itself, even anchoring itself, to the interests that will passionately and often justly oppose what the government is doing, is so apparently rewarding, that the exercise of political will lies not in going there, but in resisting the temptation to go there.

It is important to break down the logic of Blair's argument. He did not concede that the Conservative government was right. He recognized that to oppose austerity was often just. Yet the judgement on how to oppose was, for Blair, a different matter. What was at stake was Labour's right to govern a sceptical electorate.

Blair's argument is close to how Bernard Williams described the utilitarian position on moral judgements in politics. Here, the choice in question was whether or not to amplify opposition to austerity cuts, such as cuts to welfare. It included the infamous "Bedroom Tax", which reduced housing benefits for those with a spare room. Blair's argument that Labour had to convey a sense of economic competence and governing seriousness through avoiding "temptation" did not involve recognition of a moral cost. The question did not arise, because the context was what it was and Labour had to work from there to win (*ibid.*). Williams suggested a utilitarian argument that says if the choice that people may be "disinclined to do" (1981: 59) – in this instance, to not join outright opposition to austerity – is in the interest of a "greater good" (*ibid.*: 58), then such disinclination "is irrelevant" (*ibid.*: 59). The greater good in this case – getting into power through avoiding opposition for opposition's sake – was obvious for Blair, and so a moral cost did not arise. Such a position can also be understood alongside Williams' discussion of "consequentialism" and utilitarianism (Smart & Williams 1973: 82–6). Here, one can interpret a values system – in this case utilitarianism – as guiding or judging action on the basis of whether what is regarded as "intrinsically valuable" is maximized through that action (*ibid.*: 85). For a political party in opposition, often unable to prevent a bad policy being enacted by the government of the day anyway, the "consequences" being considered may then be long term and electoral; the valuable revolves around being able to govern again. Short-term opposition won't change anything, by this argument.

There are some further questions, derived from Williams, that I will not focus on here but that should be raised briefly with regard to Blair's motivations. I consider Blair's focus on governing to be sufficiently partnered with a moral claim: for example, Labour being in office would mean a greater good than the good from opposing austerity. However, there are also "claims of politics against morality" (Williams 1981: 62): in short, the motivation of power politics rather than politics for a cause. Williams noted that politicians may reach for the overarching moral claim of their party's superior values being, vaguely, the objective, and that this was a somewhat "distant" claim (*ibid.*). On these points, I adopt a more generous and flexible interpretation of the moral claims of Labour politicians considered in this chapter. Political actors being convinced – and with good cause – that achieving power would, in short order, bring about a more ethical society, often undoing specific injustices (even ones they were silent about while out of power, for fear that they were "popular"), is no small thing.

How common is this interpretation of the utilitarian view of moral judgement in Labour's politics? Let us take a more recent example, that of Labour's positioning on industrial action amid strikes over pay during the cost-of-living crisis in 2022–3. In June 2022, ahead of strikes on the railways, it was reported that a message from Keir Starmer's office had informed Labour's frontbench that the party "must show leadership and to that end, please be reminded that frontbenchers … should not be on picket lines" (Rogers 2022). In the days prior to this message, the shadow health secretary, Wes Streeting – considered to be on the party's Blairite wing – had apologized to the rest of the shadow cabinet after news coverage of his remark that, had he been a rail worker, he'd have voted to strike (Grylls 2022). Following the leader's message, the Labour frontbencher Sam Tarry – who had junior responsibility for transport – was sacked after giving media interviews from a picket line during the rail strikes. According to a leadership spokesperson, the interviews Tarry gave and the positions he took during the interview were the problem, rather than the picket line visit (Elgot 2022a). Cracks began to appear in the leadership position after this. Senior shadow cabinet member Lisa Nandy visited a picket in her constituency in a different, more local industrial dispute, leading to a brief war of words in the media (Elgot 2022b).

The journalist and broadcaster Andrew Marr asked Streeting, months later, about Labour's rather tortuous approach and comments made to Marr by US Senator Bernie Sanders about showing solidarity with workers. In response, Streeting suggested (2023) that Sanders would have lost the 2020 US presidential election, and gave a familiar response on strikes: "We're not a party of protest, we're a party that wants to be in government so we can make a difference for working people." On the basis of an understanding of moral judgement and politics, we can delve more deeply into this. The original diktat about showing "leadership" exemplified the utilitarian view. The unease within Labour at this position demonstrated that others in and around the Labour Party recognized a moral cost in not visiting picket lines, one produced by a conflict with multiple meanings associated with Labour's values: those of class, trade unionism, workers' rights, tackling economic hardship and continued inequalities, and Labour being a part of a movement (as discussed in Chapter 2).

For some, this moral cost meant finding ways of visiting a picket line anyway. For others, it meant silence, or grumbling at the leadership diktat behind closed doors, experiencing what Williams called "uncancelled moral disagreeableness" (1981: 61), which I would suggest is a relatively common experience for Labour politicians in and out of office. From Streeting came another version of the utilitarian view, with the visiting of picket lines considered the futile politics of opposition rather than the grown-up politics of government. Understood like that, there was no sense of a lingering moral cost. It was a no-brainer as to the greater good. These are day-to-day moral judgements in Labour's politics, wrapped up and obscured by political punditry focusing on tactics and personalities. They are judgements that Labour politicians wrestle with more often than not: particularly leaders, who seek to manage the different expectations used to judge whether they are "up to it" and can take "difficult decisions".

"The constraints of the job"

Ed Miliband the not very popular politician was replaced by Ed Miliband the popular podcaster and backbench MP. Why, Miliband was asked, did people perceive a different Ed Miliband as he recovered from life as leader of the opposition? The former Labour leader offered the following explanation (Campbell 2018a):

> The constraints of the job. You can't say, "Donald Trump is a moron". Even Jeremy hasn't. But also, the self-imposed constraints. I probably was too cautious. If you are Labour leader, you feel you are operating in a political war zone. There are people in the media trying to kill you every day ... So you parse every word.

Discussing the scenario of US President Donald Trump making a state visit to the UK – which happened the following year, in 2019 – Miliband stated that, freed from a leadership role, he'd be "on the demo" and would not attend any banquet held in Trump's honour. Would Miliband have attended a banquet if he'd still been a party leader? "I don't know", came the response (*ibid.*). As a politician, Miliband was and is very aware of the moral cost of political decisions, and the lingering disagreeableness that Williams wrote about. That did not mean Miliband believed it was possible to navigate politics without a moral cost. Indeed, this was something Williams also recognized. Miliband took decisions, over the course of his leadership, that people in and around the Labour Party disagreed with on principle. The key point is that, unlike with the utilitarian presumption which saw associated feelings and clashes of belief as irrelevant, Miliband sometimes struggled with these political judgements and the dilemmas they contained. A feeling that New Labour had been too quick to depart from principle affected Miliband's outlook. So too did Miliband's view of his main political opponent, Conservative Prime Minister David Cameron, who he believed was all presentation and no substance.

As Miliband ran for the Labour leadership, he took aim at what he called "traditionalist New Labour solutions on every issue" (2010b: 55). It was his "rejection of this New Labour nostalgia" that made him the "modernizing" candidate (*ibid.*, 55): because, after all, New Labour had set about discarding shibboleths and taking on conventional wisdom. To face the future, Miliband thought, Labour had to do the same to New Labour: revise it and modernize. At the root of New Labour's political strategy, according to Miliband, was pessimism. A pessimism "about the ability of our values to speak to a progressive majority in Britain" (*ibid.*: 62). New Labour had told people there was a "tension between our values and our electability" (*ibid.*: 62). Miliband posited the opposite (*ibid.*: 63): "the morally right and the electorally right thing do come together ... Head and heart come together in a politics based on clear values." Of course, positing that the right thing to do morally and politically is the same thing is not an original argument. It is also a highly convenient one and attractive to a politician appealing for the votes of Labour members who felt New Labour had gone too far and forgotten what the party was really about.

Yet as a motivation for changing Labour, Miliband was very clearly affected by it. In his address to Labour's 2010 conference, days after winning the leadership, Miliband concluded his speech with a focus on his political style. He told the audience that Labour could not "be imprisoned by focus groups" (Miliband 2010c). Instead of triangulation – not taking sides, or seeking to split the difference – Miliband promised to move on from the New Labour playbook, agreeing with policy decisions even if that meant forgoing political attacks. He pledged (*ibid.*):

[W]hen Ken Clarke [then Conservative justice secretary] says we need to look at short sentences in prison because of high re-offending rates, I'm not going to say he's soft on crime. When Theresa May [then Conservative home secretary] says we should review stop and search laws to prevent excessive use of state power, I'm not going to say she is soft on terrorism.

In the early months of Miliband's tenure, commentators questioned his chances of political success and queried whether he was establishing himself as an alternative prime minister. Then a scandal came along that spoke to Miliband's aim of challenging convention and demonstrated his capacity for political bravery. In the course of 2011, the "phone-hacking" scandal engulfed News International and Rupert Murdoch. News stories about phone hacking – where people's mobile phone voicemails had been accessed – were rumbling prior to Miliband's leadership, with questions about the *News of the World*, a Sunday tabloid, and Andy Coulson, who had edited the paper and then gone to work for David Cameron. Coulson had joined Cameron in Downing Street after the 2010 general election, and then resigned in January 2011 as coverage of phone-hacking allegations at the *News of the World* continued in *The Guardian* and other media outlets (Wintour 2011a). Coulson was later jailed, in 2014, over phone hacking. The *News of the World* stopped publishing in the summer of 2011 after it was reported that the mobile phone of 13-year-old Milly Dowler – who it was later discovered had been murdered – was hacked in 2002 by someone working for the paper when she was missing.

In the weeks after that news broke, Miliband expressed both his shock and determination to press on with a different way of doing politics. "Everything has risks in politics", he said during this period (Helm 2011). "But sometimes the biggest risk is not to take risks. You don't change things without taking risks." The risks were those taken in challenging a media giant, one subject to frequent discussion in the Labour Party. Rupert Murdoch's media titles – including *The Sun* – had a record of hostility towards the Labour Party. New Labour had sought to bring these newspapers (and others outside of the Murdoch empire) onside, with what was described as a "craven courting of editors, columnists, and proprietors [which] had long since become a source of dismay and embarrassment to many in the party" (Bale 2015: 62). Miliband, having never approved of this approach (Hasan & Macintyre 2012: 303), was clearly engaged by the idea that this insidious media and political culture might end. "So many people have believed that you can't win without Murdoch, you can't win without *The Sun*", he noted, but going forwards "the endorsement of Murdoch will be a pretty double-edged one" (Helm 2011).

Miliband saw the abuse of power within the media as part of a bigger picture, one that included his analysis of capitalism. On this optimism regarding the potential for systemic change – and as stories about phone hacking began to abate in Westminster – there were some who questioned just how shaken the political kaleidoscope really was (Behr 2011). Miliband would often remind people – in speeches and interviews – that he had shown he could do the politically brave thing with his response to phone hacking, but he had not managed to change the media and political conversation about leadership as the general election neared. In the summer of 2014, with that election less than a year away, he returned to the subject and the themes discussed above: a rejection of the utilitarian presumption and an appeal to comprehend the intellectual and moral challenges of politics. Diagnosing a cynicism within politics and the wider electorate at the prospect of change, Miliband argued that "they [the people] believe we [the politicians] value posturing more than principle ... Politics is played out as showbiz, a game, who is up and who is down ... But this political culture, this photo-op politics, denies people a debate about the things that really matter" (Miliband 2014a).

The speech was made shortly after people in the media – and people on social media – had sought to dramatize a photo of the Labour leader eating a bacon sandwich, in what will surely be looked back upon as a bizarre episode in the undermining of a politician. *The Sun* would later reuse the image in May 2015, appealing for its readers not to vote Labour. Miliband attempted to move the conversation on to his preferred political battleground: ideas. Leaders needed "big ideas to change things", he argued, along with "the sense of principle needed to stick to those beliefs and ideas even when it is hard" (*ibid.*). He recognized, too, that he didn't always make the right calls; that, at times, he had opted for a morally disagreeable position and regretted it. Noting an error of judgement in posing with a free copy of *The Sun*, released to coincide with the 2014 Fifa World Cup, Miliband argued (*ibid.*) that "sometimes you get it wrong", and that "especially for people on Merseyside, me holding up a copy of the Sun was one of those days. Politics is a hard business to get right. But consistency matters. And that means seeking to stick to your principles even when it doesn't seem fashionable to do so ... My true test of leadership is not just whether you look the part but whether you can retain your soul."

Did Miliband retain his soul? To left critics, he had some of the right motivations, but ultimately he "shared the Blairites' axioms for judging success or failure": the very who's up, who's down contest that Miliband had derided and in contrast to Jeremy Corbyn (Seymour 2016: 48). Miliband's leadership was one of "tortured timidity", according to Jones (2020: 52). Accepting the "constraints of the job" led to the idiotic "EdStone", etched with commitments derived from opinion polling. Miliband did not succeed in changing the kinds of metrics used to judge a leader and nor did he stick to them himself, largely because he did not shift the debate. He did, though, recognize the moral costs of political decisions. He did not adopt the utilitarian view, although he did sometimes opt for the "unpalatable" (Williams 1981: 58). In doing so, he attempted to move on from later New Labour.

No compromise

Of the many insights that can be drawn from Williams' understanding of a moral sensibility in politics, another is the particular vulnerabilities for a progressive party, out of power, trying to mount a political comeback and concerned about public opinion. Among the "unpalatable" acts Williams discussed, he included a "temporary coalition with the distasteful" (*ibid.*). If such a coalition were in the interests of a greater good – and for an opposition party, that greater good is often acquiring the power to make change – then an interpretation of the utilitarian might suggest such a coalition was not only necessary but that any distaste would be neither here nor there. In non-utilitarian moral thinking, and with no simple systematic framework for reaching a judgement, the moral cost of such a coalition would be one factor among others to consider when reaching a judgement. Relevant to these decisions are also political considerations, although Williams noted that the line between wanting to maintain power (which was very understandable) and the "deformation of political life", where all that matters is ambition, was sometimes hard to decipher (*ibid.*: 66).

After 2010, Conservative governments frequently sought "wedge issues" and moments – often through parliamentary votes – to place Labour in a position where it perceived both a moral cost and an electoral cost from a clash between values and public opinion. The Conservative strategy relied upon two things: that polling data could be neatly matched with a policy located within an area of public concern or popularity; and that the media would, following the first point, present such a move as politically inconvenient for the opposition, thereby maximizing the attention given to the policy (for a connected discussion of the "pollification" of politics, see Allen & Moon 2020). This was part of the plan at the end of 2012 and into 2013, when Conservative Chancellor George Osborne announced that his proposal to cut benefits would be legislated for through a "Welfare Benefits Up-rating Bill". Primary legislation was required because of Osborne's decision to limit benefit increases for future years rather than reviewing the levels each year (Kennedy *et al.* 2013). The *Financial Times* reported the news with the headline "Osborne pulls off welfare masterstroke" (Stacey 2012).

With no instantaneous answer from Labour as to how the party would vote (*ibid.*), concern from some within the party inevitably followed: would the leadership follow the utilitarian presumption and "hold its nose" while not opposing it? Or would the party recognize the moral cost as too great and duly oppose it? A letter from John McDonnell, then a backbench MP and well-known figure on the Labour left, addressed to his fellow Labour MPs was published on the website LabourList. In the letter, McDonnell (2012) argued: "I believe that we shouldn't allow ourselves to be dragged into the gutter of politics by Osborne's exploitation of the poorest ... If we have the courage and behave astutely, we could turn this cynical ploy by Osborne into an opportunity for us to transform the debate ... This means stop all hesitation on this matter."

McDonnell's suggested approach included much of what was discussed in Chapter 2: building a "coalition of all those people and organizations who are willing to speak out on what is happening to our people" (*ibid.*). Note, too, McDonnell's usage of *our* people: the communities that Labour should be representing, those who needed support and were on very low incomes. Labour needed "to highlight the real facts" about the hardship people were experiencing and to "expose this reality and offer our alternative" (*ibid.*). It is unlikely that McDonnell's intervention was decisive here. What matters more is that the general tenor of his argument was a familiar one: Labour could not support this, regardless of public opinion. To support the move would be unconscionable. Labour had to persuade people of the rightness of its approach. Within days, the Labour-friendly *Observer* had been briefed that "in a high-risk move that could define his leadership", Miliband and Labour were likely to oppose Osborne's policy. The message from those close to Miliband was similar to McDonnell's. That "his supporters believe that a broad alliance of church groups and charities, backed by Labour, could change the terms of the national debate over welfare" (Helm 2012). In January 2013, Labour MPs voted against Osborne's bill.

Jump forwards two and half years, and Miliband had recently resigned following Labour's 2015 election defeat. Labour's acting leader, Harriet Harman, was being told by pollsters that Labour had failed to regain the public's trust on the economy (Harman 2017: 350–1). People were pointing at Miliband's leadership too. And voices from the New Labour years expressed sorrow at Miliband's decision to attempt to move on from New Labour, having adopted what some saw as an oppositional approach. Peter Mandelson told the *Andrew Marr Show* that Labour's strategy under Miliband had been wrong-headed (Mandelson 2015): "in a sense we were sent off in 2010 on the sort of giant political experiment in which we were ... told to sort of wave our fists ... angrily at the nasty Tories and wait for the public to realize how much they missed us".

Osborne, meanwhile, was back with a new welfare measure, including a lower "welfare cap". While overseeing an election for a new leader, Harman announced on the BBC that Labour would not oppose the bill, nor the proposed lower cap. The public, Harman said, didn't want to see "blanket opposition" from Labour (Harman 2015). This bill, she believed, had to be used to show an instant response from the Labour Party to the electorate. Harman's message was met with dismay by many within the party and a parliamentary rebellion. In the knowledge that Labour's frontbench "reasoned amendment" to reject the bill in favour of a different approach would fail, the party opted to abstain on whether the bill should proceed. Among the leadership candidates, only Jeremy Corbyn voted against rather than abstaining, joining a rebellion of 48 Labour MPs (Demianyk

2015). John McDonnell said in the House of Commons debate that he "would swim through vomit to vote against this Bill" (Hansard HC Deb, 20 July 2015). Corbyn's campaign, meanwhile, located Labour's turmoil in a wider narrative about failing to stand up to austerity (Demianyk 2015). For Corbyn supporters, Harman's decision added further momentum to their candidate's campaign (Nunns 2018: 170–1). Harman later reflected that Corbyn's candidacy acted as an outlet for those fed up with Labour's direction (2017: 350):

> There had been tensions in the party since the start of the Blair years that we were not progressive enough ... but our being in power and then, after 2010, our hoping to get back into power, had masked that ... Jeremy's candidature gave vent to those feelings. The public had gone in one direction and the party was setting off in the opposite one.

We now know that, unbeknownst to Harman at the time, Labour was perhaps already fighting yesterday's battle. According to the British Social Attitudes Survey (Butt *et al.* 2022: 18), public opinion on "tax and spend" – whether governments should increase taxes and public spending, keep them the same or reduce them – was starting to change at this point. With support for increases having steadily reduced in the run-up to the global financial crisis in 2008 and immediately after, 2015 saw support for increases start to significantly rise again. By 2017, 60 per cent of people said the government should increase taxes and spending on health, education and social benefits, compared to 33 per cent for keeping them the same and 4 per cent for reducing them, support for which has been consistently low over the years (*ibid.*). By the high watermark of Corbynism – the 2017 election result – Corbyn's supporters could plausibly claim that his political stances opposing austerity, and rejecting other moments where Labour had seemed to compromise on its principles (campaign mugs with Miliband's election pledges, including "Controls on Immigration", for example), showed that Labour had been too quick to concede the political argument. However, a new moral and political dilemma was about to dominate British politics.

"Loud and proud in support of Europe"

Labour's deputy leader from 2015 to 2019, Tom Watson, had an eclectic career at the top of Labour. Often associated with the parliamentary unrest that eventually led to Tony Blair setting an exit date as prime minister, Watson eventually emerged – paradoxically – as a political figure seeking to reconcile Labour's warring factions after Corbyn's 2015 leadership triumph. Having stood down as an MP at the 2019 election, Watson later revealed how he perceived the political mood in 2015, noting (Hattenstone 2019): "We [Corbyn and Watson] had just won the leader and deputy leader ballots, and we were in this room on our own, and the first thing he said to me was, 'we've got our party back.'"

Watson didn't feel the same way and was reluctant to turn on the party's record in office (*ibid.*). While previously close to senior figures from the trade union Unite, who would become some of Corbyn's strongest supporters, Watson soon found himself attempting to shape, but simultaneously rise above, the events that rocked the Labour Party: from leadership challenges to Corbyn to political strategy. By 2019, any working connection between the deputy leader and the leadership had disappeared. In the June of that year, with Labour debating its position on Brexit vociferously and a political crunch coming, Watson delivered a speech that targeted Corbyn's supreme unease about Labour and Brexit. Labour's members were overwhelmingly in favour of staying in the EU. A political fight seemed to be on for Britain's future, one based on big, principled arguments about being in or out of Europe. So where on earth, some people wondered, was Jeremy Corbyn? Was he, as some charged, "fence-sitting" when he should have been confronting "the threat of Nigel Farage" (Toynbee 2019)? Sensitive to the political mood, Watson said that the EU was "not something to apologise for". It was in step with Labour's values and not something that should be reluctantly accepted, as Corbyn was widely perceived to have done. He told a pro-EU think tank (Watson 2019): "Brexit is not a brake on Labour values. It is an existential threat to them ... Our members are remain. Our values are remain. Our hearts are remain. We need our Labour Party to be true to who we are and be loud and proud in support of Europe."

For Watson, that meant the party campaigning for a referendum as the only option to end the political quagmire and rising Eurosceptic populism. In a referendum, Watson argued, "the party of socialism" had to be campaigning for Europe. He ended the speech by asserting (*ibid.*): "The patriotic choice is to remain."

There was understandable disquiet among the party leadership at the speech (Pogrund & Maguire 2020: 236–7), and events snowballed over the following months, culminating in a botched attempt at Labour's 2019 conference to abolish Watson's job. However, rather than organizational intrigue, what matters for the argument presented here is that Corbyn was in a position where internal critics could plausibly argue that Labour's principles were being compromised. Watson's language was deepest red and unapologetically pro-European, not the contradiction in terms some of Corbyn's longstanding allies believed it to be. In addition to the grumpiness at undermining Corbyn's authority, the rhetoric hurt because it revealed that Corbyn and his team had adopted the utilitarian presumption: that the moral cost of Brexit was a price worth paying if it achieved a Corbyn government. Unfortunately for the leadership, that greater good argument was looking highly questionable, as the strategy of refusing to take a side moved from being plausible (a couple of years earlier) to being doomed. For Owen Jones, a high-profile Corbyn-supporting columnist, while Watson's rhetoric on socialist principle was overblown, the ambiguity at the heart of Labour on the biggest issue of the day was not sustainable. While recognizing the electoral dilemma for Labour MPs in Leave seats, Jones countered (2019):

> For too many others, a false dichotomy that pits "working-class leaver" against "middle-class remainer" distorts their analysis. They look at centrist, London-based remain leaders – some of whom have cynically used Brexit to undermine the Labour leadership (disillusioned members of the People's Vote campaign openly tell me that Blairites have used the issue to regain political relevance) – and extrapolate.

In making his case, Jones touched on two important, interlocking elements to explain Corbyn's reluctance to embrace a pro-European position: the Labour Party's renewed sense of commitment to class politics, and – once again – Blairites. This was a powerful blend of meanings that some within the Corbyn project could not disentangle. One long-time Corbyn ally, and then aide, derided anti-Brexit campaigning as "Brexit Derangement Syndrome" that could "destroy" Corbyn's voter coalition (Murray 2019: 214). For "Love Corbyn, Hate Brexit" supporters, there were more overtly left anti-Brexit campaigns to associate with, so the leading People's Vote campaign – with its backers including Tony Blair, Alastair Campbell and Peter Mandelson – could be ignored, sidestepped, accommodated or worked with in the interests of stopping Brexit. As the quotation from Jones above inferred, for other Corbyn backers there was anger and cynicism at enthusiastic referendum supporters – many of who did not agree with Corbyn's overall political approach – criticizing Labour for triangulation (being neither Remain nor Leave). This was, after all, what Corbyn supporters had criticized previous Labour leaderships for. As Corbyn sceptics derided the then Labour leader for not making up his mind, wasn't there more than a hint of *Schadenfreude*?

And then there was Labour's "return to class" (Pike & Diamond 2021: 671–3). Corbyn had argued that "for 30 years, the media and the establishment tried to tell us that class doesn't matter anymore" (2018). Part of Corbyn's project was to push back against this viewpoint. Laura Pidcock, the former MP for North-West Durham, who held the seat from 2017 to 2019, had been chosen by Corbyn to head up a Ministry for Employment Rights if Labour won in 2019. Pidcock argued, in her time as an MP, for a clearer class politics. Corbyn's changes had meant, she argued, that Labour would "go into a general election to speak for our class" (Pidcock 2019), a change from the Thatcher–Blair consensus where "talking about class in political circles was almost taboo" and "class considered an anachronism" (*ibid.*). This was not a new interpretation of New Labour, and – as with Pidcock's general argument – there is some substance to the view. Analysts have pointed to the modernization process – culminating in New Labour – to explain the weakening of working-class support for Labour, with former voters initially choosing not to vote, before finding alternatives (Evans & Tilley 2017). This was not, according to Evans and Tilley, because the (admittedly much smaller than in the mid-twentieth century) working class no longer existed, but because political parties (including Labour) had changed: there was policy convergence among the main parties, and changes to party identities and style (*ibid.*: 163).

Labour, so this argument goes, opted to move away from a part of its identity being the representation of the working class. In doing so, some working-class people judged the party as no longer representing them and didn't vote for them (*ibid.*: 176). There were warnings, too, from work undertaken during the New Labour years (Seyd & Whiteley 2002: 181). Without relitigating the debate here, there are a number of responses to this narrative. For example, whether New Labour had much of a choice in appealing to a middle class that held the place in British politics the working class once did: in other words, the largest group of voters (Savage 2017: 708). Regardless, the pegs securing Tony Blair's "big tent" politics were gradually unearthed over time, in part for contingent reasons, in part owing to longer-term trends interacting with party strategy, as existing analysis has shown (Evans & Tilley 2017; Sobolewska & Ford 2020).

More pertinent for the argument of this chapter – and this book – is how different judgements were reached when faced with a very real "Brexit dilemma". Some Corbyn-supporting MPs from Leave seats were angry at the idea of a referendum (Pogrund & Maguire 2020: 135), seeing it as aloof, arrogant politics overturning a huge exercise in democracy, and one linked to an institution that Corbyn and many of his backers didn't have much love for anyway. Corbyn's team had successfully swerved Brexit in the 2017 election and appeared to resent being drawn into a politics they did not choose. For some in the leadership, Brexit politics threatened the prospect of a Corbyn government, through the loss of Labour's Leave seats and working-class heartlands, and conflicted with Labour's "return to class". Yet many in and around the Labour Party not only disagreed with the electoral calculation – pointing to Remain voters who could also be lost – but perceived a very different moral cost: a Conservative and Nigel Farage-inspired political project that was nationalist in character and economically ruinous in outcome (including for Labour's heartlands). In short, a political tragedy that had to be opposed. As politics became Brexit-obsessed, not picking a side could feel wrong (Toynbee 2019).

Having awarded the EU "seven, or seven and a half out of ten" on TV during the referendum campaign, appeared to call for the immediate triggering of Article 50 and then prevaricated on Labour's vision for Brexit (e.g. the customs union or the single market) and on a referendum, Corbyn seemed oblivious to the principles at stake. I don't believe that Corbyn, or his team, were purely motivated by politics, because the potential election of a Corbyn government – for his supporters – was seen as a moral victory in itself. What was remarkable was the often bewildering ambivalence to the moral costs of accepting Brexit, despite knowing full well that "Lexit" – the shorthand for a "left Brexit" – was a relatively rare passion within Labour and not something many of those in and around the Labour Party would be convinced by. In the short-lived climate of people thinking that Brexit could be stopped, the perceived absence of the Labour leader appeared to clash with Labour's values.

Who is Keir Starmer?

Leaders of the opposition get a lot of advice, which is one small part of what makes the job unenviable. With very little to comment on in the form of actual things being changed in the world – because the leader is not in government – leaders of the opposition find every small decision they make subject to a court of commentators, who note the strategic nous or electoral ineptitude of every twist and turn (even when the public have not noticed anything). Take the following advice from Janan Ganesh (2023), a columnist for the *Financial Times*:

> The soft leftists are the people that Starmer has to upset … only when he is resented by most of his own party will swing voters believe he is a true moderate. This means telling trade unions that structural reform, not just spending restraint, is coming to public services. It means a clearer and more traditional line on the culture wars.

The "soft left" – a label applied to an often large group of Labour MPs (and people in the party more widely) who find themselves in the middle of the party – were identified by Ganesh as people too often worried about being "bad guys". This explained, he argued, why the public support Labour leaders "from the very right of the party", such as Blair (*ibid.*), and not soft left politicians. We see here the danger of putting people into very broad categories that tell us something but don't really explain much. Replace a fear of being the bad guys with an understanding of moral costs in politics, and we get closer to comprehending why political commentators – including Ganesh – can sometimes criticize Labour politicians for hesitation. They do indeed, as Ganesh suggested, worry about doing bad things. Yet considering moral judgements, rather than placing people into categories, also takes us to the flaws in this critique: should moral cost always be dismissed in favour of electoral motivation? Is ruthlessness without morals a political virtue? Is that what people join the Labour Party for? Critics may not approve of the traditions and beliefs of the institution, but this may be because they understand the purpose of politics very differently. At best, arguments of this kind can embody the worst of utilitarian thinking: chastising those who recognize moral costs outside of a simple argument for the greater good. At worst, such an argument risks swerving morality entirely and be focused only on political power. As Williams argued about utilitarianism, this might give decision-makers "less to worry about", yet such a "minimal commitment is not enticing" (Smart & Williams 1973: 137).

Some senior figures from the New Labour years have been keen to point to a significant political fact over the last decade and more of opposition: "The last 11 general elections read 'lose, lose, lose, lose, Blair, Blair, Blair, lose, lose, lose, lose'", Peter Mandelson has said (Cheng-Morris 2021). Yet others, such as the MP Jon Cruddas, who worked for Blair during the early New Labour years, have argued that the "Blair, Blair, Blair" winning sequence was far from one simple story. Indeed, the first victory – at least – involved a Blair more clearly connected to an ethical socialism (Cruddas 2021: 150). Reflecting on Blair's role in crafting his own political legacy, Cruddas argued that Blair had "consciously buried his early political character" (*ibid.*): "It is almost as if it is too painful for him to return to the source of his emotional power and success. It amounts to self-harm in the way he diminishes who he once was."

Starmer has found himself caught in these battles over New Labour. Should he follow the advice of some commentators who – it should be recognized – have offered arguments similar to those elaborated by Blair after Labour left office in 2010? Or should he be wary of an approach which embraced the utilitarian presumption much too strongly and evaded moral dilemmas that had a real impact on the party and its politics? These are connected to perhaps the biggest question yet asked about Starmer as a leader: what does he believe in? I noted in Chapter 1 that some of Starmer's commitments have been readily made and just as readily jettisoned. These are often rational decisions if one considers the utilitarian presumption. Starmer's leadership so far suggests he has embraced this outlook.

Anyone who has tuned in, even briefly, to a Keir Starmer speech since 2021 will probably have heard the Labour leader talk about his family: his parents in particular. He has often noted that he does not come from a "privileged background", that his father was a toolmaker and his mother a nurse. Take, for example, his first in-person conference speech as leader, after the easing of pandemic restrictions (Starmer 2021c):

> [W]hen I hear that this country is creating so many low-paid jobs and when I tell you that good work and fair growth will be the priority for a Labour government, I haven't learnt this in some political seminar. I learnt it round the kitchen table. I learnt it at home, from my dad. How pride derives from work.

In the party's 2022 annual gathering, Starmer repeated much of this, something he does regularly in his speeches to communicate what is, for him today, a key message (Starmer 2022): "you may have heard some of this before. I grew up in a pebble-dashed semi. Dad was a toolmaker, Mum was a nurse, our first car was a Ford Cortina – this was the 1970s." He described his approach to leadership as one driven by "working class impatience": that "if you're born without privilege, you don't have time for messing around" (*ibid.*). Starmer's pitch has a core motivation, but it is also affected by different things. On the motivation, his aim is to communicate a sense of ordinariness that some people may not jump to when considering his career as a senior – and knighted – public servant. Starmer's record as a human rights lawyer, who wrote regularly about the law and challenges of defending and extending rights, has been seized upon by the Conservative Party, who have attempted a rather desperate "leftie lawyer" attack on the Labour leader, presumably on the basis of populist logic that Starmer can be portrayed as part of an out-of-touch elite. Starmer's backstory directly challenges this, presenting a meritocratic story that speaks to Labour's past too. Starmer's approach to other issues speaks to another narrative of class politics as well, one summed up by Alan Johnson, the former Labour MP, in a critique of Corbynism (Chesterton 2020): "The main problem was their [the Corbyn project's] lack of patriotism, the kind of thing the far left can never ever connect with [the] working class over. There is a part of the far left that despises working class culture."

Part of Starmer's leadership has been about reaffirming a particular interpretation of working-class "patriotism", which he has connected with moving on from the Corbyn period. Starmer wrote in *The Times* (2023b): "The Labour Party I lead is patriotic. It is a party of public service, not protest. It is a party of equality, justice and fairness; one that proudly puts the needs of working people above any fringe interest. It is a party that doesn't just talk about change – it delivers it."

Much of this rhetoric from Starmer is unsurprising and associated with some essential – although incomplete – changes that Starmer has made to Labour. In addition to party reform, Starmer has returned some Labour positioning and rhetoric to a very recognizable Labour tradition. Similarly, stressing Starmer's successful legal career as something achieved through hard work is a part of his story and tells voters something about his personality and character. What is more interesting, and important for understanding the question mark over

Starmer's leadership for many, is that in the past he has viewed the compulsory sharing of a backstory as strange, and once credited to Corbyn – and John McDonnell – the achievement of "making us more comfortable with [a] radical vision" (Kale 2020). On the backstory, Starmer told a journalist during the 2020 Labour leadership election that (*ibid.*): "The idea that a person who's been in a professional career for years – in his 50s – now has to tell people what his mum and dad did, is odd." Yet he has embraced the habit because he wants to repel Conservative attacks and become prime minister.

Does Starmer believe that his background is important to his politics – that "working-class impatience" – or does he think it is odd to remind voters in numerous interviews what his parents did for a living? As I noted earlier in this book, because jettisoning commitments has itself become a habit for Starmer, the idea that he says one thing and thinks another has been something his critics have honed in on. Starmer said in 2020 that Labour had to make the argument for free movement with the EU, yet as leader he ruled it out (Crerar 2022). To what extent does he believe in either position? When the then chancellor, Rishi Sunak, was reported to be increasing corporation tax in 2021, Labour appeared to see an opportunity to outflank the Conservatives on business taxes, before backing the move and defending it after Liz Truss's short-lived scrapping of the rise. There are arguments that can be made for many of these changes, yet they need to be considered as an overall approach to leadership. Understood more critically, Starmer's leadership has been incredibly tactical, looking for the short-term gain with each and every decision and sometimes leading to inconsistency, as with the case of corporation tax. The amount of tax corporations should pay is not merely a tactical decision in the up and down game of Westminster politics, it is a decision that should rest on an ideological foundation.

The clash between values – and what Labour "really believes" – with Starmer's strategy to become prime minister was clear in a row over a Labour attack on the Conservatives that appeared on Twitter (now X) in early April 2023. Labour tweeted an image of the prime minister, Rishi Sunak, with the headline text: "Do you think adults convicted of sexually assaulting children should go to prison? Rishi Sunak doesn't" (Labour Party 2023b). A political furore followed. Joining criticism from the Labour left (McDonnell 2023), David Blunkett, a former Labour home secretary under Blair – and no stranger to communicating messages on law and order – said it was "deeply offensive to get down in the gutter to fight politics" that way (2023). Starmer defended the messaging in an article, saying that he stood "by every word Labour has said on the subject, no matter how squeamish it might make some feel" (Starmer 2023e). Equally revealing was the response from some Labour figures regarding Yvette Cooper, the shadow home secretary, after reports that she had not been involved in agreeing the advert. One "insider" unleashed a rant to the *Daily Mail*, saying that "if Yvette disagrees so strongly with pointing out the Tories' dismal record on crime, she knows where the door is" (Owen & Hodges 2023).

In targeting people who felt "squeamish", Starmer was raising the issue of people feeling a moral repugnance when seeing the advert. In his argument, the controversial rhetoric was defensible because behind crime figures was real suffering by real victims of crime who had been let down by a system that wasn't working very well and, presumably, could only be fixed by Labour. The insider comment to the media took that approach further, positing politics over morals. The whole episode was also, as Andrew Marr pointed out during the row, a hideously macho approach, "a laddishness, a self-delighted savagery … which brings to mind the worst of the Alastair Campbell era" (Marr 2023). During the row over the advert, the case was made by some that aggressive attack politics was necessary and that the Tories always did it to Labour. Unease at the advert was presented as being naïve and failing to understand "real politics". Labour had to play the game and cause some offence. One Labour figure told *The Times* that the ad "was a deliberate plan to be provocative and disruptive and, to be honest, I don't think anyone thought it would work this well" (Dathan 2023). Here, the politics is all. The achievement was the creation of a row. At such an early stage, no evidence as to the political efficacy of the strategy was available, so insiders asserted its relevance and tactical nous in an evidence-free vacuum.

Reflecting on his leadership overall, Starmer suggested he had needed "complete ruthlessness" (Zeffman 2023). Starmer has often been ruthless, yet at times he has also appeared rudderless. Ruthlessness partnered with progressive conviction can be a powerful political force for Labour and has been – at times – for Starmer. Ruthlessness without conviction leads to questions about a lack of principles and accusations of "flip-flopping". Starmer's passion for fixing things can only be harnessed if he has a steady gaze on what those problems are. When people have suggested that Starmer isn't straightforwardly political – as previous aides have done (Dickson & Webber 2023) – they have typically meant that he has had a long a career out of politics and is therefore somehow above the Labour political scuffle. Yet this description applies much more widely. Starmer is political in the sense that he wants to run a government and the country, changing institutions and leading offices of state. He is decidedly less political in believing in a cause and in recognizing the kind of political conduct which can lead people on the left to hesitate. If Starmer becomes prime minister, this will be written up as a great strength, until the ideological choices of government swiftly become front and centre, when it risks becoming a weakness. From opposition to government, the "utilitarian presumption" appears far less simple, and much harder to defend. The immediate costs of political judgements will be Labour's responsibility.

Conclusion

In the penultimate season of the fictional US TV show *The West Wing*, veteran political advisor Josh Lyman (played by Bradley Whitford) embarked upon an insurgent campaign for congressman Matthew Santos (played by Jimmy Smits) to be the Democratic nominee for president. The campaign struggled for airtime in the media, other candidates ignored them and congressman Santos found himself locked out of the only chance to debate his competitors at the start of the primaries. Lyman suggested an attack ad, one portraying the other candidates as "chicken" for not debating Santos. The candidate viewed the video and was not amused. After some soul-searching, the congressman opted to walk into a television studio for his one-minute advert and talk to the camera about a more grown-up, serious politics; a politics where, if the candidate wants to criticize something, he says it himself. He literally dropped the (very small lapel) microphone and walked off the set, revitalizing his campaign in the process as media outlets rushed to replay this untypical ad. Chickens chasing political opponents is of Labour vintage, too. So is the dream of the soul-searching candidate who changes the rules of the game.

If one were to imagine the response of the three Labour leaders considered in this book to the fictional scene above, I think it would go something like this: Miliband would see a kindred spirit but worry about the risk; Corbyn would agree with the general thrust of changing politics for the better but mention that Matthew Santos had compromised on too many political positions in an unforgivable manner; and Starmer would suggest that, while admirable, the whole thing was a bit naïve and he was more focused on getting things done. The argument about Labour's political style is as old as the party, and made worse by the caricatures that this chapter has sought to move beyond. No leader considered in this chapter offered an approach that always took the "principled" Labour view. On Europe, it's possible to make an argument that having never really believed in the EU, even on that issue Corbyn stuck to his principles and fought to hold a more sceptical line. But the job of being a Labour leader is never solely an individual pursuit. When a party perceives a leader not sticking to principle, its members can often be projecting their own principles. In prevaricating on Europe, Corbyn collided with the party's beliefs.

Ruthlessness in politics is sometimes understood as prioritizing what appears to be in a politician's interest at a certain moment in time. With Starmer, that has meant wholly committing to something, or wholly rejecting something, depending on the leadership's reading of the immediate political circumstances, and forgetting that what is being wholly committed to or rejected should, ideally, stand the test of time. In the political moment, it is easy to forget how contingent and contextualized politics so often is. Liz Truss' first and only fiscal event – the "mini budget" of 2022 – was hailed by some in the media as necessary economic medicine until people swiftly awoke to the painful consequences, and then her time as prime minister was up. Political leaders must be mindful of political fashion but not too dedicated to it. Undoubtedly, since 2010, there have been many moments when the Labour Party has failed to reach appropriate judgements. Yet the story of the last decade is more than these errors. At times, it has involved people in and around the Labour Party facing up to complex political problems and trying to make the right call. The difference I have elaborated in this chapter is entirely about recognizing that many of these decisions have a moral cost. In other words, they are not simple ones.

That isn't to say decisions shouldn't be taken – decisions in politics can rarely be avoided for long. Nor is it to say that Labour's politics can be conducted with no moral costs, as compared to a kind of politics that appears not to care at all. And it must certainly not be read as a form of "moral self-indulgence"; that is, where a person cares "not so much [about] other people, as himself caring about other people" (Williams 1981: 45). Williams' essential argument, which has inspired much of the analysis in this chapter, is that politicians who do recognize moral costs may be more likely to avoid unnecessary ones in their political decision-making (*ibid.*: 62). I suspect this is right. The alternative approach, which one can find in Williams' critique of utilitarianism, is an overconfident one and is intrinsic to a political style that leaves too much of what is bad about politics still in place.

4
MOVING ON: LABOUR'S DEMOCRATIC SOCIALISM

Introduction

Chapters 1–3 have argued that since 2010, the Labour Party has reached important judgements about its political direction on the basis of what its leaders – and a wider group of people in and around the Labour Party – thought about New Labour. On ideology, the party rediscovered ideological debate and enhanced the significance of confronting inequality within the party's ideology. In relation to democracy, the party turned against "machine" politics and, while not always succeeding, arrived at a vision for greater community participation. And with politics, the party saw the need for a rebalance between the electoral imperative and political conviction. Since 2015, something of a counter-reaction has been underway. Keir Starmer's leadership has been far less critical of New Labour, sometimes with just cause. Part of Starmer's strategy to distance his project from the Corbyn years has been a rejection of attacking New Labour and an embrace of some of its famous rhetoric. But a difference of interpretation when it comes to New Labour – and a difference in reaction – is not the same thing as a readoption of New Labour's politics. Starmer's Labour is not a New Labour tribute act, certainly not in substance, which is near impossible when the world has changed so much anyway (Garland & Pike 2023: 9). More precision is required in drawing comparisons, which I attempted in Chapter 3 with the more specific idea of a shared "utilitarian presumption".

What is the ideology of Starmer's Labour? This chapter locates the contemporary Labour Party in a simultaneously recognizable yet amorphous political tradition: something called "labourism". Labourism has had a number of critical definitions thrust upon it over past decades (Shaw 2004). For Marxist critics, labourism stood in lieu of a full-throated socialism propagated both inside and outside of parliament (Miliband 1972: 331–2). For critics of a more social democratic disposition, labourism was constituted in part by the conservatism of the British labour and trade union movement and reluctant to embrace ideas outside of this narrow tradition (Marquand 1999: 17–25). I define labourism in one form that takes something from both of these critiques: it does not set a clear direction towards the "good society". This omission always betrays a lack of confidence. When Labour lapses into something close to labourism, it is neither clear nor confident in its ideological objective. "Equality" gives way to a vague expression of "fairness". When Eric Hobsbawm wrote that "Labour is not and cannot be just a party which offers the voters a better deal than the competition does on, say, pensions and bus services. It offers a good society" (1989: 220), he hit the nail on the head with regard to a certain understanding of labourism: it offers a better deal, but it does not say this is the society we hope for and must work towards (*ibid.*).

With Keir Starmer located within the tradition of labourism, that he has very often changed his mind and rethought his priorities is unsurprising, because to offer a better deal is both relative and reactive. The contemporary Labour Party's ideology is a mixed bag. The party will head into the next general election (likely to be in 2024) with some radical, progressive policies that could tackle injustices within British society and improve life chances. Yet a clear sense of direction is not the driving force behind the presence of those policies. To reiterate, Starmer's labourism is not seeking to replicate New Labour. Nor is it a policy vacuum. Rachel Reeves, as Starmer's shadow chancellor, has sought to align her political economy with that of President Joe Biden's in the United States, endorsing US Treasury Secretary Janet Yellen's thinking around "modern supply-side economics". As discussed in Chapter 2, growing the British economy outside of London and the south-east, and a focus on regional economic inequality, is also an important part of Starmer's labourism. Both of these points stress a more "active" state in Labour's political economy. They also include Labour's leadership giving voice to a political difference from New Labour and the politics of the 1980s and 1990s. In my view, Labour does not offer merely the status quo, but nor does it have a clear sense of where the country should go and what the good society looks like.

My argument in this chapter, informed by the analyses in preceding chapters, is that Labour can and should adopt a much clearer set of ideological objectives. If it did, its ideology would be less of a mixed bag and its actors less uncertain, which are important things for any future Labour government. I draw upon the three themes of this book in setting out this form of democratic socialism or social democracy: both terms, I think, can apply here. The first section of the chapter offers a brief précis of Starmer's labourism and, through a critique, begins to make the case for a clearer ideological position. In the second section I discuss works of political theory that contain insights for what ideological clarity can bring and what socialism can be. The third and final section of the chapter sketches out what this could mean in practice. Here, I make a brief programmatic case and an argument for a different kind of Labour politics. Throughout the chapter, I draw contrasts with labourism and engage with the context of our times and the ideological strands that have cohered around left politics.

This is an optimistic chapter. It also presents what social scientists some-times call a "normative" view about politics: in other words, as well as analysing what is happening, I say what I would prefer to happen. Labour is, as the party constitution says, a democratic socialist political party. Previous chapters have highlighted ideas integral to what that means. It is an ideology that is, funda-mentally, about all of us: the "social" bit. It isn't about any one bottom line, nor pursuing one dominant way of life. Democratic socialists aspire to a society where people are treated as equals and can flourish in their own way, believing, too, that through acting together we are more likely to advance towards those objectives. The "democratic" bit is not limited to the constitutional principle of a free democracy, although that is essential. Democratic socialists seek ways to share power more widely and – if people want it – to empower people to take more decisions that affect them and their communities. Finally, to advocate for democratic socialism is to challenge and change the rules of the game. In part, that can be achieved through greater equality and democratic practice: the first two central components of democratic socialism. But it also means being brave in political style, always seeing the bigger picture and conducting politics in a way that recognizes the moral matters of every political judgement. This chapter makes a case for such a politics.

Labourism

The term "labourism" is far from ideal. I have much sympathy for Eric Shaw's argument (2004: 201) that labourism, when historicized, does not appear to mean much at all. The key problem is when labourism is considered to be – even if by inference – "causal": in other words, that *because* of an ideology and a culture called "labourism", the Labour Party is almost uniquely disappoint-ing among the social democratic family (Marquand 1999: 17). When applied in broad brushstrokes to depict Labour's history, Shaw is right to see it give "rise to over-simplified, over-generalized and in some cases simply erroneous views" about the party (2004: 201). I don't think labourism explains – in any simple sense – Keir Starmer's emerging reputation as a political chameleon, nor do I think it can be used to explain a century of (often) political crisis and defeat for Labour. Instead, I see it as a recognizable tradition within the Labour Party, one that can be affected by Labour politicians and others in and around the party (on traditions, see Bevir 2011: 12). It is a tradition that can change over time, all the while carrying meanings from one generation to the next that contain a certain plausibility: that Labour is not a talking shop, that it too often becomes absorbed in abstract debates and that it should instead look to apply values such as fairness in the circumstances of the time. Added to this is a recognition of Labour's working-class connection, with its origins in the trade union movement and continued relationship with organized labour. This latter point is something that appeared to be disappearing during New Labour (Shaw 2004: 202) but has made a comeback.

Labourism, then, is not a catch-all causal factor, nor an explanatory term that has as wide applicability as some scholars have suggested. But it remains a useful characterization of a tradition – among others – within Labour. And it helps us to understand the kind of ideological positioning Keir Starmer has arrived at (Manwaring *et al.* 2023). In his May 2023 speech to the Labour group Progressive Britain – a rebrand for the previous group Progress, which stemmed from the New Labour modernization years – Starmer made some headlines by invoking memories of Tony Blair's revision of clause IV, the part of Labour's constitution which details the party's objectives. Blair, famously, substituted a new ideological statement for the previous commitment to some form of common ownership. Starmer suggested his task was to go "further and deeper than New Labour's rewriting of clause IV". For those glancing at the morning headlines, this no doubt appeared as more affiliation with New Labour rhetoric, attempting to build an association with successful political times, and this was probably part of the motivation. But when listened to and read, Starmer's speech was subtler and more nuanced in relation to New Labour.

His central message, while seemingly in keeping with Blair rhetorically, was that Labour had to "reconnect" with "working people". "It all boils down to this", Starmer said (2023h):

> [T]he Labour Party will only restore hope in the country, if we once again become the natural vehicle for working people ... Some people think all we're doing is distancing ourselves from the previous regime. We are – but that misses the point. This is about taking our party back to where we belong and where we should always have been, back doing what we were created to do. We've been drifting away from working people for a long time – and that's unforgivable ... Who are we in it for? Who do we serve? Who do we wake up in the morning and fight for? Who do we have in our mind's eye when we make decisions?

As noted in Chapter 3, a critique of New Labour's distancing from class politics was not only influential after 2010 but also had some substance. Starmer subsequently framed Corbynism as being out of touch with one interpretation of working-class politics, owing in particular to a hesitancy over "patriotism". But in carefully noting that the accumulation of distance between Labour and "working people" had been happening for "a long time", Starmer also connected his argument with other threads this book has discussed, including Lisa Nandy's argument about New Labour's embrace of globalization. Starmer noted that he was "not afraid to use the language of take back control", the Vote Leave slogan that Westminster politicians and commentators have accepted into political campaigning folklore as a formidable rhetorical weapon. Starmer's appetite for reforming the state, he claimed, supported his strategic objective (*ibid.*): "Seriously – walk round any working class community and you will be hit over the head by this. The people we need to serve no longer have faith in an unreformed state."

Starmer's speech also attracted comment for a section laying claim to "stability" and the importance of "conserving", the latter topic associated with the Blue Labour project discussed in earlier chapters. Labour's predilection for radical change, he argued, "must never become unmoored from working peoples' need for stability, for order, security" (*ibid.*):

> If that sounds conservative, then let me tell you: I don't care ... The Conservative Party can no longer claim to be conservative. It conserves nothing of value – not our rivers and seas, not our NHS or BBC, not our families, not our nation ... the lesson for progressives must be that if a tide of change threatens to sweep away the stability working people need, we have to be in there – fighting for security just as fervently as we fight against injustice.

Labourism is not, in any simple way, the "cause" of this political language. Starmer's positioning – as I made clear in previous chapters – has been highly contingent. In the above speech he was reacting to political threats (the spectre of Brexit) and real failures of Conservative governments (sewage in rivers) that have been notable since he became leader. Yet as a descriptive tool, labourism is a good fit for Starmer's rhetoric. Labour taking its lead from the people's priorities, and balancing its progressive urge with some kind of innate conservatism, can be squarely located within the tradition of labourism. In other words, there exists a Labour home for Starmer's cautious and technocratic instincts.

If we remind ourselves of some of Labour's policy platform, we arrive at something close to labourism too. In previous chapters I looked at the party's devolution agenda and its "new deal for working people". These ambitious measures have been partnered with C/conservatism (arguably mostly lowercase "c") in other areas, most notably on moves away from tax reform and on caution around public spending. They add up to the potential for better terms and conditions in the workplace, and the creation of new jobs – if private investment also returns – over the medium term. But in seeing Starmerism through the labourist lens, we also see a contradiction at its heart. It is a good political argument to suggest that the Conservative Party has failed to conserve what it set out, in 2010, to maintain. It has not secured Britain's economic future, the NHS has been left in crisis and Britain has struggled with problems tackled or resolved more swiftly elsewhere: polluted rivers or expensive and unreliable transport connections for instance.

But there is also a contradiction here. If something has not been conserved, and so much is broken, then what are you conserving? For example, if the NHS is in crisis – which many people accept has been the case in recent years – and needs resources and reform, you will be looking to raise more money and to change how things work. You will not be seeking to conserve, nor even to return to a status quo from the past, because so much is changing and public services need more resources and new thinking. In short, you are in the change business, not the conserving business. On one level this can be dismissed as semantics: can we not understand "Conservatism" as restoring something to a better position and "conservatism" as simply the politics of reassurance? But I think it is far more than semantics. Labour is partly in reassurance mode because it is fearful of Conservatism (with a capital "C" for the most part) in two ways: it is fearful that, despite giving the country four prime ministers between 2019 and 2022 and showing all the signs of a political party that has lost any fundamental orientation, the Conservative Party can still deprive Labour of power and limit any time in power that Labour enjoys. And it is fearful that, connected to the first fear, the strength of Conservatism (and conservatism) in Brexit-supporting England will mean a sceptical electorate hesitating for much too long before supporting Labour.

On the first fear, Rishi Sunak taking over from Liz Truss may not result, the political scientist Tim Bale has argued (2023: 291), in the Conservative Party abandoning right-wing populism:

> [A]nyone hoping that, under Sunak, they [the Conservatives] will downplay the culture war strategy so evident under Boris Johnson is likely to be sorely disappointed … rather than the installation of a supposedly more "technocratic" Cabinet halting and even reversing any transformation on the part of the Conservative Party from a mainstream centre-right formation into an ersatz radical right-wing populist outfit, it could … just as easily accelerate and accentuate it.

Labour has responded defensively in this regard, rather than putting forward a competing Labour case. Take, for instance, the topic of migration. Starmer's rhetoric has demonstrated his wish to attack the Conservatives, hoping – no doubt – that vociferous rhetoric will prevent the Conservatives from succeeding with the strategy summarized by Bale. In a session of prime minister's questions, Starmer directed the following at Sunak (Hansard HC Deb, 24 May 2023): "They have lost control of the economy, they have lost control of public services and now they have lost control of immigration. If the prime minister was serious about weaning his government off the immigration lever, he would get serious about wages in Britain and get serious about skills and training."

This is political attack wrought in part by a fear that the Conservatives could use right-wing populism to cling on to power. Following on closely from the argument of Chapter 3, critics could point out that Starmer is failing to recognize the moral costs of responding to Conservative strategy with very Conservative rhetoric about losing control of immigration. Starmer may well, as the speech quoted earlier noted, believe the rhetorical power of "take back control" to be formidable, but his political attack is itself predicated on the notion that the Conservatives have played with fire and misled people about migration. The same risks are faced by the Labour Party.

There is a wider, dangerous politics here too. As Aditya Chakrabortty observed, in Britain "the air is once again poisonous. Far-right groups have been visiting accommodation for asylum seekers, trying to terrify those inside" (2023). There is a long history of racist responses to migration into Britain. At best, some Conservative politicians have chosen to ignore this history, and some of the consequences we have seen in the past. The Brexit referendum campaign was enveloped by this kind of politics. We see it whenever people arrive in the United Kingdom to claim asylum, having paid smugglers for passage in the absence of any accessible kind of safe and legal route. The responsibility politicians should be required to exercise in their language cannot be overstated. There is not, and has never been, an "invasion", which was the Conservative Home Secretary Suella Braverman's language (Hansard HC Deb, 31 October 2022). People are not a "swarm", a word used by David Cameron when prime minister (Elgot & Taylor 2015). That a country should have an asylum and immigration system, with a process for granting protection and with visas issued for people coming and going, is comprehensible enough. But too little is known about how cruel that system can be to people who have very little – those fleeing persecution or conflict, for example – and how often it simply does not function properly. The migration system is in one sense a bureaucracy like any other, but it sits within a politics of racism, populist demagoguery and scapegoating. Labour's job is to challenge and change that politics.

The second, connected fear is about the perceived strength of C/conservatism within the UK, principally in England. This is epitomized by some of the less sophisticated analysis about the Red Wall seats Labour lost in previous elections. But it is also related to longstanding beliefs about Labour's electoral coalition, as well as a certain pessimism from very different Labour traditions:

that Labour has never been liberal enough (missing out on the progressive coalition) or is never C/conservative enough. The progressive intellectual and former Labour MP David Marquand once wrote that in the twentieth century, "Liberal England may have died, but Labour England has failed to be born" (1999: 9). For Marquand, this was in part owing to the culture of labourism. He lamented Conservative hegemony in England, and he thought aloud about an alternative history: one where Lloyd George and "New Liberalism" was not eclipsed by Labour and the Conservatives but managed to survive the tribulations of the Great War, and afterwards introduced something close to a "New Deal" society or even Scandinavian-style social democracy (*ibid.*: 17). Instead, Labour had struggled to assert itself and the Conservative Party dominated twentieth-century British politics (*ibid.*: 25).

From a very different political standpoint – a Blue Labour position very critical of liberalism – comes a similar despair at Labour's lack of ideological imagination, but with a different outcome in mind (conservatism pushing out liberalism). Jonathan Rutherford, who worked with Maurice Glasman on the Blue Labour project, responded to the speech from Starmer (cited above) with the following argument (Rutherford 2023): "Starmer is cautiously ending the liberal progressive politics that has dominated the Labour Party for three decades … The future will be about stability and security … restoring and conserving the things that matter to people."

Rutherford's list for conserving included "cultural values", good jobs, safe streets, "reducing immigration" and "respect for authority" (*ibid.*). Blue Labour thinkers have sought to find connections to this kind of political project in Labour's past, which is certainly possible, and surely nobody would be against good jobs or safe streets. But is this package ideologically distinctive, let alone preferable for Labour as a democratic socialist party? It certainly combines labourism with C/conservatism. Yet, as a result, it appears to have little to say about the policies and the politics that could rescue Britain's public services, face up to the climate crisis and create a more equal society. That is the case that should be made and from where Labour must win. As those three things – the state of public services, facing up to the climate crisis and creating a more equal society – are the most important challenges facing a socialist or social democratic project in Britain today, Labour needs to look elsewhere: beyond labourism, and beyond C/conservativism, for ideological renewal.

Thinking about socialism

Something that Labour's critics often cohere around is the diagnosis of a lack of an alternative: that Labour doesn't have a sufficiently clear view of the good society. To this, I would add that Labour's ideology needs a greater sense of ambition. That isn't to say that Labour's programme must promise all things in a short time frame. Rather, it means its ideology – and its overarching goals – must be ambitious for the longer term, while a Labour government makes meaningful reforms as it progresses. This is critical to overcoming hesitancy and a lack of confidence. This is always important, but consider Labour's current context: the party will have been out of power for nearly a decade and a half by the next election. David Cameron memorably noted, when he stood in Downing Street having become prime minister, that New Labour had made the country "more open at home and more compassionate abroad" (Cameron 2010). It is hard to see how a future Labour prime minister could return the complement. The record of the Cameron years can obviously be debated, yet there are few measures to accompany equal marriage on a list of solid accomplishments. After Brexit – a choice that Cameron offered through a referendum – came consecutive political meltdowns, including a former prime minister, Boris Johnson, being found to have lied to parliament. While a party's electoral challenge is always of great importance, and some humility is often in order, ideologically the Labour Party needs to have much more confidence that it has better answers than its political opponents.

Different thinkers have stressed the point about ambitious overarching goals as one of the benefits of a coherent ideology. For Elizabeth Anderson, ideologies "are vehicles for our hopes and dreams … [they] function as *ideals*, offering us not only representations of the world as it is, but as it attractively *could be* if certain actions were undertaken" (2017: xxi, emphasis in original). In a discussion about utopias and dystopias, Mary Midgley said much the same as Anderson. For Midgley, conceptual maps – guides akin to ideologies and other forms of vision – "must bring forward the central issues, making them look clear and limited enough to tackle. They must also envisage distant possibilities which haven't yet been considered" (Midgley 2000: 16). In short, here is what we can do now, and here is where we plan on going. It is on these thoughts – and others like them – that a belief in the necessity of a coherent, confident ideology rests. Does Labour have an ideology to act, as Anderson said, as a "vehicle for our hopes and dreams"? It undoubtedly has elements of a vision, which is most clearly articulated in its economic policy and in Labour's commitment to addressing the climate emergency.

In the first half of 2023, the shadow chancellor Rachel Reeves visited the USA to both further substantiate and consolidate the ideological affinity between Labour and President Biden's Democratic administration. In a pamphlet published to coincide with the visit, Reeves committed to "a new business model for Britain that follows the 'modern supply side' approach. It is one that will make us stronger and more resilient in an uncertain world, and help us seize the opportunities of the future, like clean energy, artificial intelligence and life sciences" (2023: 6).

The term "modern supply side" comes from US Treasury Secretary Janet Yellen, who seized the idea of supply-side reform from the political right – who often associate it with deregulation and tax cuts – and instead associated it with reforms that expand and improve a country's productive potential. The connection with tackling the climate emergency is important. "Essentially," Yellen said, "we aren't just focused on achieving a high topline growth number that is unsustainable – we are instead aiming for growth that is inclusive and green" (Lawder & Shalal 2022). Such a focus isn't entirely new within the political economy of the left (Murphy 2023b). It is reminiscent, too, of Gordon Brown's rhetoric of avoiding "boom and bust": in other words, not seeking to get the economy moving for a few years, only to see the stimulant for that growth overheat or cause some other market response that results in a bust.

Yet, in both the US and British contexts, the Democrats and Labour are seeking to present this approach as a change from "Third Way" 1990s social democracy too. In a 2023 speech, the White House national security advisor added further thoughts on the Biden–Yellen agenda. The era of globalization – and liberal economic reforms from the 1980s onwards – had worked on the assumption that "the type of [economic] growth did not matter. All growth was good growth … Our industrial capacity … took a real hit" (Sullivan 2023). Not only that, but inequality went unchecked (*ibid.*). From the US perspective, modern supply-side theory has also clearly developed within in a much-changed diplomatic and policy context in relation to China: supply chain security, a presence in green industrial production (e.g. electric car batteries) and a strategy attempting to learn from the outcomes of previous approaches to international trade have all featured (*ibid.*). Reeves embraced a criticism of globalization too. Modern supply side meant the end for globalization as we had known it, with a different comprehension leading to new strategies and political ideas (2023: 30).

Reeves called this approach, based on modern supply-side theory, "securonomics". An economist in the United States, Dani Rodrik, has called it "productivism". For Rodrik, "there are signs of a major reorientation in economic policy – one that is rooted in production, work, and localism instead of finance, consumerism, and globalism. And it might turn into a new paradigm that captures the imagination of both sides of the political spectrum" (2023: 9).

As a new economic paradigm, this broad approach – with its many labels – can undoubtedly contribute to a coherent political economy for Labour. Rodrik's version of productivism is alert to regional economic inequality and complements the diagnosis of some Labour politicians, as discussed in Chapter 2. And the necessity of the green transition – alongside the undoubted effect of a different diplomatic posture in relation to China – means there is a clear emphasis on the "onshoring" of production. Reeves has consistently made this point since becoming shadow chancellor. Rodrik contributed something else, though, which is pertinent to the matter of an overarching ideology. He suggested, understandably, that paradigms are contingent and context-specific: that what works in economic policy today may not work tomorrow (Rodrik 2023: 10). "The keywords of a truly useful economics", he wrote, "are contingency, contextuality, non-universality" (*ibid.*: 9–10).

In other words, what we have here is a political economy of means geared towards a fairer kind of economic growth, influenced – certainly within the US administration – by developments in global diplomacy and power. For Labour, that is part of the story. But it is not an ideology. It does not present overarching ends, particularly in relation to the choices that need to be made about the state of Britain's public services and the reforms that are necessary to bring about a more equal society. To achieve social democratic or socialist ends, for example, will require redistribution through the tax and welfare systems. In that sense, productivism as a paradigm should not be expected to provide too much direction for Labour. It marks a shift in political economy, but Labour will continue to require greater clarity over ends. Anyone familiar with social democracy will know about the longstanding debate over means and ends: the debate is as old as what we understand contemporary social democracy to be (Plant 2004: 106). In short, ends could be enduring and speak to long-held socialist and social democratic goals. Means needed to be flexible. And the context, for socialist and social democratic parties, was one of party competition, electoral arithmetic and appeal beyond the working class (Esping-Andersen 1985: 6–10; Przeworski 1985: 34–8).

This was central to social democratic "revisionism" in nineteenth-century European social democracy and later into the twentieth century. In Plant's words (2004: 106): "Ends were permanent; means were contextual." This takes me to the contemporary debate. This distinction – between means and ends – has been breaking down within Labour for some time. Plant powerfully argued that New Labour had made much of the distinction between means and ends to connect with Labour's past revisionists, and to make the case for the continuity of ends (e.g. more social justice, just like with the "old") but driven by a "new" political economy (2004: 113). Yet certain means were apparently ruled out, and other means preferred, all within the context of globalization. Plant wrote (2004: 118–19):

> If the argument against going further, by for example taxing top incomes, is ruled out on grounds of the knock-on effects on incentives and competitiveness in a global economy then it seems to me that we have to accept that the policy restrictions imposed by globalization etc.

have so constrained what is politically feasible that the conception of equality embodied in Labour's history has been reinterpreted in the light of this.

In other words, if the means become relatively fixed, political options become limited, so limiting the ends you can aim for. We have seen much the same with Keir Starmer's leadership, with a whittling away at the distinction. Keir Starmer has ruled out a sequence of measures to bring about tax fairness, in favour of other means to achieve just outcomes – namely growth and predistribution policies. Reform in public services, while necessarily part of the conversation, has become a political priority in and of itself: in other words an end, seen as preferable to having to spend more money. This limitation in terms of means clearly affects ends. And as we have seen, productivism – or securonomics – perhaps sheds some of the perceived economic curtailments of globalization, but it does not purport to be an ideology. More work, then, is required to prevent means displacing ends and a resultant narrowing of Labour's political ambition.

Before sketching out some ideas for Labour today, I conclude this section by considering some socialist political theory alongside the distinction of means and ends. Both G. A. Cohen and Axel Honneth (two thinkers who have been compared recently, e.g. Piromalli 2020), considered how we conceive of socialism, what we are seeking to achieve with it and the political practices required to move towards it. To begin with Cohen, we have a conception of socialism as an alternative form of social relations: something I noted in the introduction and think is incredibly important for Labour's ideology. Cohen used an analogy for understanding socialism: a camping trip. He sketched out a recognizable experience of going camping with people and generally acting in an egalitarian way: if food is acquired, it is shared, so too the tasks that campers need to carry out (2009: 3–6). These things are not done according to market principles: nobody is saying, sure, I have some surplus toilet paper (let's accept this is a camping trip with communal toilet facilities provided), but it seems that overall there is a shortage of toilet paper among our group, so I'll be charging 50 pence a sheet. Of course, as Cohen recognized, society doesn't function like a camping trip. In a smaller group of people you know, what you are prepared to share may be different. And as a camping trip is a micro social case, focused on a particular social circumstance, what does this really tell us?

The key point of Cohen's argument, from my reading, is that what motivates the manners and decorum of this social occasion – and others like them – is that people act on the basis that to share and work together is the norm, and nobody feels that they are having their freedom curtailed nor that they are being treated unfairly. As Cohen wrote (2009: 43): "The relationship between us under communal reciprocity is not the market-instrumental one in which I give because I get, but the noninstrumental one in which I give because you need, or want, and in which I expect a comparable generosity from you."

In short, to cooperate and act within a socialist logic "does not require me to be a sucker" (*ibid.*: 43). Instead, society operates with the shared social logic of support rather than the market logic of giving to receive. If that approach is the norm in some of our activities together, running through the same logic in more of our activities together is at least possible. Therefore, increasing the forms of activity in life that work with this alternative, non-market social logic matters for socialism. Cohen arrived at this point following a discussion of inequality, and an argument that suggested too great an extent of inequality of outcome (which is possible even with a commitment to equality of opportunity) puts the exist- ence of community in peril, because we live very different lives on the basis of varied financial power (*ibid.*: 24–36). A final point to take from Cohen is about political practice. The stumbling block to socialism is not, Cohen argued, one of right or wrong principles; it is that we have not worked out an economic system to deliver the "communal reciprocity" model advocated above (*ibid.*: 58).

Honneth's argument was based less on a form of moral theory and thought experiments and more on a particular kind of political practice: what he called "experimental" socialism (2017: 74). Yet there are similarities in Cohen's and Honneth's conceptions of socialism. The latter found in the work of early social- ist thinkers much elaboration of the concept of "community", understood "not just as a set of shared values and a certain degree of identification with the aims of the group, but primarily as a feeling of mutual responsibility and sympathy" (2017: 23). Honneth took this as the kernel of socialism. To this he then added thoughts inspired by the philosophy of John Dewey, particularly Dewey's focus on democracy as a way of life and of expanding our shared experiences (Dewey 2008a: 93), and elements of philosophical "pragmatism", specifically that social theories are to be shaped by the world and that forms of "social action" – for example, reforms and practices – were to "be treated as working hypotheses, not as programs to be rigidly adhered to and executed" (Dewey 2008b: 362). These two insights were combined by Honneth to create the experimental model of socialism. He wrote that "socialism must be viewed as the specific modern ar- ticulation of the fact that in the course of history and on the basis of varying social circumstances, new groups constantly seek to draw public attention to their own demands by attempting to tear down barriers to communication and thereby expand the space of social freedom" (2017: 65).

Returning to ends and means, for Honneth you should not lose sight of your goal, but nor should you conceive of that end being brought about through one dramatic socialist heave. Instead, you do things that you believe contribute to- wards the goal and you try them (*ibid.*: 69). The source of hope is not theory per se, and not materialist comprehensions of economic and social affairs, but instead "the traces of social progress in whose realization socialism has played such a decisive role for 200 years" (*ibid.*: 106).

There is a Deweyan point that both Cohen and Honneth offered – although it is more implicit in the former – and that is Dewey's emphasis on participation, practice and experience: the trying of something and observing its effect (2008a: 146). In education and learning, for example, "making the individual a sharer or partner in the associated activity so that he feels its success as his success, its failure as his failure, is the completing step" (*ibid.*: 18). In Dewey's thinking, society exists through communication and the sharing of ways of doing things (*ibid.*: 7). So much, then, of life and progress exists through communicating and through shared experience. That leads to Honneth's conclusion that socialism should be about all citizens – not a particular class – and that socialists can prove the efficacy of the ideology through reforms in our shared society (2017: 74). This kind of thinking is also at work in Cohen's argument that if we look around us, we see social practices – at least in some instances – where market logic does not dictate choices. "Doctors, nurses, teachers and others do not, or do not comprehensively, gauge what they do in their jobs according to the amount of money they're likely to get", Cohen argued (2009: 59). In other words, there are "very definite moral limits to markets" (Plant 1984: 14) in our everyday lives, and they are a product both of our beliefs and of our experience.

The point of Cohen's camping trip analogy was to bring our experience into contact with theory, another similarity with Dewey (2008a: 151). We can illustrate the importance of this shared philosophical insight to socialism with a contemporary UK example. The NHS is much talked about in the UK, evoking the language of religion and ideology. As Polly Toynbee wrote (2018):

> When Nigel Lawson [a Conservative chancellor during the Margaret Thatcher years] called the NHS "the closest thing the English people have to a religion", he said it with sneering despair: why is this usually Conservative-leaning nation so stubborn in its NHS adoration? But the party's leaders know they tamper at their peril with one of our island story's key creeds, one that inspires authentic patriotism.

Socialists and social democrats could do worse than think about why Lawson was allegedly in despair at these circumstances, and why Toynbee could plausibly make this argument about the NHS. Others have suggested that while the NHS was "one of the single greatest achievements of any Labour government in history", it was not a socialist policy (Blakeley 2021). Here the focus is on the forces of labour and capital, and the state acting in the interests of the status quo and therefore the latter. State institutions tackling inequalities may be social democracy, but they are not socialism (*ibid.*). Przeworski argued much the same when he suggested that "Mitigation does not become transformation: indeed, without transformation the need to mitigate becomes eternal" (1985: 41). Yet if we adopt the conception of socialism from Cohen and Honneth we would, I think, consider the NHS to be a very important socialist policy; one that, if built upon, would be playing a part in a gradual transformation. Why? Because the NHS shapes social relations in a non-market-oriented way. And related to Toynbee's summary of love for the NHS, the health service provides a non-market experience in our day-to-day lives. If it works well – and this is a very important if – then it can create and maintain a belief in the efficacy and morality of socialist practice. The building of such institutions, and the spreading of democratic practices in different areas of society and life, takes us further towards a socialist or social democratic way of life. This needs to feature much more within Labour's ideology as an overarching end and socialist objective.

Labour's democratic socialism

In 1984, with Labour having suffered a second defeat to Margaret Thatcher's Conservatives the previous year and still riven with factional infighting, Stuart Hall wrote that people still did not seem to understand the scale of the problem facing Labour. It was not an instance of a couple of bad electoral defeats, important though that was. Rather, the "underlying consensus in the political culture around the historic compromise struck in the post-war years, which had underpinned British politics and which gave Labour its legitimate claims of office" had gone (Hall 2017: 209). Putting to one side historical debates regarding the presence (or not) of a postwar consensus, Hall was right that the 1980s were to be grim years for Labour nationally. He was also right, at least in terms of effect, that something had unravelled, something else was being made, and all of that changed the political environment of Britain. Jump forwards to today and things are looking much better, electorally, for Labour after a similarly grim decade where much has unravelled and things are very changed. Some have suggested this is a similar moment to that which Hall talked about, but with the political parties switched and the Conservatives on the slide: "1979 reversed" (Toynbee 2023).

Yet it does not currently feel like that. In this final section I make some suggestions for how Labour could create something new. That means a more coherent policy agenda to tackle the three big challenges the country faces: the state of public services, facing up to the climate crisis and creating a more equal society. On the last challenge, that means Labour properly comprehending the intersectionality of inequality, including the relationship between inequalities of class, race and gender. It means rethinking the role of a political party in the context of a significant redistribution of power away from Westminster. And it involves recognizing that in politics choices can be very hard but must be confronted. It is tempting to suggest to a tired and concerned electorate that the current management has run things into a wall and a change in management will fix a lot of things. Starmer's real interest in changing the state might make some difference on that point. But it would be disingenuous to lay everything at the door of poor management and poor judgement, not least because both rest upon political beliefs. One of the virtues of a more coherent, ideological approach to politics is that challenging those beliefs is a priority. Such an approach is evident at times, particularly regarding Labour's green investment plans.

When Keir Starmer set out Labour's climate mission (2023i), which I discussed in Chapter 1, he was at his most emphatic on the clash between different political philosophies, buoyed, no doubt, by a general mood of acceptance at the Biden administration's own green investment policies. "When the winds of change are blowing this fiercely," he argued, "you need a government that gets involved and intervenes … this is about Tory ideology … They still cleave to the set of ideas that came out of the 1980s … the contempt for active government … these ideas are finished." Labour's investment, clarified in 2023 (and with a provisional air into 2024) at £28 billion a year by the second half of the next parliament, is the centre not only of its climate mission but of its economic growth plan. It is worth dwelling on two particular ideas Labour has put forward for how to spend that money: the creation of what the party has called GB Energy, a company owned by the state which will "own, manage and operate energy generation projects" (Labour Party 2023c: 16), and a new National Wealth Fund that will invest in green industries, like electric car battery factories (*ibid.*: 5). Both are public investment programmes, but the detail of how they will operate is of real interest, including for thinking through the challenges and priorities discussed above. With GB Energy, the plan is to make private investment in clean energy more attractive through public investment, "derisking" such investments and encouraging new jobs within the UK. With the National Wealth Fund, Labour has said that it wants "the British taxpayer … [to] get a return on its investment and where appropriate, own a share of the project to ensure it happens" (*ibid.*: 18).

According to the think tank Common Wealth, the prospects for such plans – albeit with heftier investment – would be significant, although *how* Labour envisages the ownership model is crucial (Brusseler 2023). In relation to the National Wealth Fund, two examples illustrate the importance of the details. First, as well as an equity stake – that is the government owning some of a company that is has invested in – what plans does Labour have for a future say in how those companies operate? (*ibid.*). Second, how could the state's (possible) return on investment be used (*ibid.*)? Here is where ideology comes in. Returns could be used, alongside investment from the state, to help integrate the green transition both with protecting public services and creating a more equal society. As well as the creation of new jobs – potentially through a guaranteed job programme, as discussed by Atkinson (2015: 144–5) – distributed around the country and tackling regional economic inequality, further investments could be made in social enterprises working to alleviate fuel poverty (e.g. through free or very low-cost installations of green alternatives), for example. Such an approach would also support the creation of institutions operating with a different, non-market social logic.

In other areas of policy, Starmer's approach – as discussed in previous chapters – has been more defensive. On Brexit, Starmer has remained somewhat circumspect, although MPs such as Stella Creasy are beginning to make the case for bolder change (Creasy 2023). That change is essential. It may have felt politically astute – and, let's be honest, easier – to say very little about Brexit in the aftermath of the 2019 election. However, as the economic hit sinks in, changing Britain's relationship with the EU may end up being the biggest political effort of a future Labour government. On tax, the Labour's leader's strategy has gone far beyond circumspect. Instead, he has gone out of his way to rule things out (see Chapter 1), painting a future Labour government into a corner when the state clearly requires more money. The Labour leadership has opted to defend – albeit with some built-in flexibility on timing – its green investment but clamped down in other areas. This has led to some flip-flopping, for example a short-lived commitment to "universal childcare" (Stacey & Mason 2023).

Labour's fear – as with the £28 billion in green capital investment – is that the Conservatives will attack Labour for borrowing more money (at increased cost compared to the post-financial crisis years, owing to the rising cost of borrowing), pushing up inflation and ultimately harming households through overspending and fiscal mismanagement. On this point, we can refer back to the fear of Conservatism argument above. This attack could, of course, also be levelled at the Conservative Party which did, during Liz Truss' brief period as prime minister, seek to increase borrowing not for capital investment but to fund tax cuts while maintaining levels of public spending, something which coincided with market chaos and a shock to some household finances. There is an important distinction – a market narrative if you like – between what happened during the Truss government and borrowing to invest in the green transition. However, the point I wish to make is that there is an alternative to Truss' plan for borrowing to fund day-to-day spending (which something such as childcare reform would require): tax.

In the early part of 2021, with the world still reeling from the effects of the Covid pandemic, the International Monetary Fund made headlines by calling for increased taxation of wealth to help fund recovery, mentioning – among other things – higher taxes on capital gains (Elliot 2021). As noted in Chapter 1, the non-alignment of rates of income and capital gains tax was strongly hinted at by the shadow chancellor as something Labour could reform. The party then backed away from it. Yet ensuring someone pays the same rate of tax on the profit from selling shares as someone pays on their salary earnings would raise a significant amount of money each year (see Duncan 2021; Hunsaker 2023). There are other options too, of course, to tax wealth and income from wealth, either through one-off measures or permanent reforms. More broadly, Starmer ruling out changes to capital gains tax signals a reluctance to consider significant tax reform, despite both the necessity of tax reform to the public finances and what we know about the contribution of taxation to tackling economic inequality.

Not only that: without raising revenue, policy innovation becomes less likely. Labour at the UK government level could embrace innovative policies, testing their efficacy and pushing towards a more equal society. Take Labour in Wales, where – if properly evaluated – we will soon learn about the impact of a basic income for young adults leaving care. No Labour politician would deny that institutions created to foster increased sociality and solidarity have been hit hard by austerity. Getting serious about tax is essential to addressing this, as well as to providing funding for new ideas that could create a more equal society. Again, we come back to the importance of a coherent, confident ideological outlook: to challenge Conservatism (and conservatism), to prioritize (even when under political pressure) and to keep in mind the ideals that explain why a political party is in the business of politics in the first place. A future Labour government seeking to (mostly) maintain the status quo – and Starmer's self-imposed constraints on tax – will come under great pressure.

Labour needs to embrace a different kind of role for a political party too, and a different political style than it has adopted of late. On the first point, and as I discussed in Chapter 2, Labour's ambitious plans for decentralizing and devolving power could be of real political significance, bringing resources and decision-making much closer to local communities. This calls for a lot of democratic thinking, particularly around the involvement of people in local communities, and requires not only "consultative" involvement but a prioritization and decision-making role. But the point I want to touch on here is about the Labour Party itself and how integrated with local communities it really is. A point about its candidates for political office is illustrative. Labour wants to be the party of public services, but how realistic is it for a nurse, or a teacher, who relies on their salary and has caring responsibilities to become a candidate for political office? Not very, is the short answer. Labour's process for selecting parliamentary candidates, for example, can be both incredibly time-consuming and expensive. There are some good reasons for at least the former: party members who spend

lots of their free time campaigning for their local party deserve time with prospective candidates before voting for somebody.

There is no good reason for the latter, and indeed the expense is linked to
the former. Prospective candidates take significant chunks of time off work,
sometimes to travel to different parts of the country to introduce themselves,
and spend some time getting to know people. Candidates produce online videos
and literature. They have numerous cups of tea and chats with local members,
seeking their votes. Only some people have the time and money to do these
things, and many of them are already members of the political class (Allen 2018:
9). If the Labour Party in office is to give power away – decentralizing it, not
only from Whitehall but also local council offices – then as a party it needs to be
constituted by the people in those communities across England, Scotland and
Wales. A renewed grassroots party is essential to holding local office holders,
with increased powers, to account. And Labour needs to go the extra mile to
ensure that, wherever possible, it acts to increase the democratic participation
of people who often face time and resource pressures: pressures that prevent an
enhanced contribution to democratic and political life. Trade unions are very
important in this regard, but of course not everyone is in a union. Labour, currently, is still too closed off.

Finally, on political style, a response to the dilemmas and issues raised in
Chapter 3 – the moral cost of politics – is to start levelling with the public more.
Politics is hard. There are rarely easy choices, and bravado doesn't get you very
far when it comes to policy change. When faced with electoral dilemmas and
sceptical responses from voters, people in and around Labour have on occasion
turned to two (equally ineffective) opposing strategies: vapid managerialism or a
belief that saying something has won an argument. Both strategies are self-com-
forting. Practitioners of the former tell themselves they are undertaking serious
politics and know how to win elections; advocates of the latter tell themselves
that through the issuing of a press release or the making of a speech their argument has probably changed people's minds. Yet political parties – and their
politicians – are not, for the most part, aloof. Many people within them are clear
in their motivations and serious about their political objectives. They also know
that they need consent for their political plans: they need to win elections, win
arguments and secure lasting support for their proposals. Doing so, as we have
seen through some of the events discussed in this book, means that political
actors perceive constraints on what they can and cannot do.

I think people outside of politics understand this better than politicians
sometimes assume. Eric Hobsbawm, in his famous "Forward March of Labour
Halted?" lecture, told his fellow Marxists that a movement must "formulate not
only what we would want to do, but what can be done" (1989: 22). This became a leitmotif in Hobsbawm's political writings (Pike & Diamond 2020: 763).

Hobsbawm's socialism was simultaneously idealistic and realist. His political ire was directed both at ideological timidity and at "sectarians" fighting their own party colleagues as much as the Conservatives (Hobsbawm 1989: 96). This kind of stance can be maddening for some people in and around the Labour Party, mostly those who do not like the word "ideology" or those who engage in factionalism. To critics it is paradoxical at best, trying to have the best of both worlds. But more likely is that Hobsbawm proposed – to adopt a suitably Marxist term – a dialectic: that of idealism and the conditions of the moment producing a purposeful yet viable politics. It isn't about the either/or but the interaction between the two. Nor it is a strategy for "splitting the difference": that is too blunt. What Hobsbawm had in mind was more nuanced.

The Brexit referendum was a big democratic exercise that resulted in much political upheaval and the creation of political identities – Remain and Leave – that defined the 2019 general election and played a key part in reshaping Britain's electoral geography. It's possible to make a similar observation about the 2014 referendum on Scottish independence. Yet on both topics, things are now starting to look different again. On Brexit, public opinion has become more negative about the decision to leave (Larik *et al.* 2022). Opinion polling in the summer of 2023 suggested the political hegemony of the SNP was ending (Nutt 2023). There appears to be caution within the Starmer project about being too bold and an inclination to rule out risk, not only electorally but with people's sense of risk, which lies behind Starmer's security narrative. Yet compared to the two referendums considered above, a bolder offer for stronger public services, an effective response to climate change and efforts to bring about a more equal society is nothing like the leap in the dark embraced by the SNP and Vote Leave. The public may, rightly, be suspicious of a magic bullet for solving Britain's problems, so Starmer's Labour should not offer one. Instead, they should talk honestly to the public about Britain's problems and make it clear what they think is possible and how. The public may be more receptive to good ideas than Labour seems to think, making the kind of purposeful but viable politics Hobsbawm had in mind very possible. As Ben Jackson argued (2022): "It should be possible to find a few ambitious, but deliverable, reforms that would both give a clear boost to egalitarian aims *and* Labour's electoral prospects."

Conclusion

Life is not a game, Raymond Geuss argued. Games are for fun and are not serious – even the most competitive among us would probably accept games are not *that* serious – and often have clear rules that are written down. Life is not like that, Geuss noted. It is not always fun, it often involves the serious and there isn't a rule book (2020: 83). What about politics? There can be moments of joy and pleasure, but I'm not sure that anyone could credibly describe it as fun. Politics can be surreal and very silly. But most of the time it is incredibly serious. And it does not have a rule book, so it seems that politics – unsurprisingly, as a part of life – is not a game. It's the last point – the idea of a rule book – that I wish to conclude this chapter with. The idea of rules – constraints, prevailing beliefs or tests that politicians are asked to meet – has been ever present in this book. Indeed, I've used the shorthand of the "rules of the game" myself, noting that Labour should push back on some of them. For constraints or prevailing beliefs contrary to our own matter a great deal in politics. There is a risk, though, that people within political parties – particularly ones that have lost so many elections – forget that prevailing beliefs are not actually rules. Unlike the rules of Scrabble, prevailing beliefs change, informal rules can be challenged – fairly – and they are not understood in isolation but in a wider context of many beliefs and priorities.

I do not wish to sound naïve or to indulge in a kind of political optimism that pretends our own beliefs are all that matters in electoral politics. Rather, Labour – the people in and around it, collectively – is in danger of codifying interpretations (and overinterpretations) of politics which have shown varying levels of validity and may now be wrong. Political caution on taxation is understandable. On that, Labour looks to experience and the fear of Conservative attack. But there is no credible rule to suggest that Labour should be as defensive as it is. On Brexit, the prevailing beliefs – politically embodied not only in the 52 per cent to 48 per cent but in Labour's 2019 electoral disaster – are now changing, some would say faster than Labour's perception of the state of play. And on the state of public services, the rule that says reform is always smarter politics than providing more resources is in dire need of some contextualization. One of the benefits of a coherent and confident ideology is that the rules of politics – the prevailing beliefs we can perceive as constraints – can be more regularly queried and tested. That does not guarantee that they can be ignored. But it does make for a more restless and reforming government.

CONCLUSION

Has the Labour Party gotten over New Labour? I think the answer to that is "no", although much has changed over the last decade or more. This book has shown just how impactful interpretations of New Labour and its legacy have been for the contemporary Labour Party, across ideology, conceptions of democracy and the right way to reach political judgements. The word "impactful" is operating as an umbrella term here, beneath which are an array of interpretations about the consequences. It is possible to argue, for instance, that the impact of the dominant (negative) interpretations of New Labour has been disruptive and damaging. It is also possible to suggest the still semi-hagiographic view of New Labour has had a stultifying effect, obscuring for people in and around the Labour Party how to confront today's political experience, rather than that of the 1990s and early 2000s. I have no doubt that these kinds of arguments – and others like them – will continue to be made in and around the Labour Party, but something has changed in post-Brexit Britain: there has been a little more acknowledgement of complexity, contingency and nuance when it comes to New Labour. To return to the question of whether Labour has gotten over New Labour, we can break it down into two broad parts: the historical take on the New Labour project and the New Labour governments; and New Labour as a touchstone. In this concluding chapter, I bring together the different threads of this book's argument, all with relevance to these two parts of the New Labour conundrum.

On the historical take, I suggest the context in which New Labour has been – and is being – thought and written about matters, and that today there is a reassessment underway. This is not about writing out New Labour's mistakes, but nor is it about writing off New Labour's achievements either. Rather, it is to reinterpret New Labour at a greater distance and with the comparator of successive Conservative governments. On New Labour as a touchstone – a kind of orientation point from which to judge the good and the bad within the Labour Party – I argue that while this is connected to the historical assessment of New Labour, it can be understood as a distinct thing in itself and has arguably been the more damaging part of this debate. It has contributed to entrenched factionalism and ugly politics. Aspects of "New Labour as a touchstone" remain present in and around the party. Finally, I discuss something that partly explains why – possibly for the foreseeable future – New Labour and its legacy will remain important in contemporary Labour politics: that is the current conjuncture where, for different reasons, the politics of the 1990s, trade liberalization, an embrace of globalization and the role of the state are subject to renewed focus within left politics. This is happening in the United States, where people in the Democratic Party and within the Biden administration have – in rhetoric and policy – moved away from that period in significant ways. Through the impact of "Bidenomics", and through a longer-term narrative within the UK, including the loss of the Red Wall, Labour is doing much the same.

The past and New Labour

On the historical take – and by that I mean the opinion everyone in and around Labour has about New Labour, informed by experience as much as by what they have read and watched – New Labour remains an object of fascination. As an academic, there is always the risk that because you are aware of mostly academic histories and works of political science about New Labour, you think it is more an object of fascination than it actually is. But stepping outside of academic debate and publishing, albeit still within the world of politicians, political commentary and opinion, you can still appreciate the volume – and frequency – of historical interest. When the former shadow chancellor, John McDonnell, went on the BBC to protest what he alleged was Keir Starmer's purge of the Labour left, the first question put to him on camera was a comparison to Tony Blair and New Labour: Blair had got on well with left-wing firebrand Dennis Skinner, journalist Nick Watt suggested, and had "tolerated" the Labour left. McDonnell readily agreed (BBC 2023b).

Starmer regularly finds himself compared, typically unsympathetically, to Blair in terms of leadership style and attributes (Beckett 2023). The "will he be a Blair?" question about Starmer is an unsurprising one, perhaps. At its simplest, it asks whether the person wanting to be Labour's next prime minister will be like the last-but-one Labour prime minister. But I think the historical interest goes much deeper, and for some good reasons. When the Conservative Party passed the point, in 2023, of having occupied office longer than New Labour did between 1997 and 2010, it felt natural to compare the Conservative record to Labour's comparable stretch in government: as noted in Chapter 4, the comparison is not a positive one for the Conservative Party, so why shouldn't we continue to be interested in Labour's longest-serving government that achieved a pretty long list of solid achievements?

Of course, the opposite case is also valid: one focusing on New Labour's mistakes. Nobody (I assume) is still angry about the Millennium Dome. It no longer feels important. The same cannot be said for many other New Labour mistakes. Instead, people in and around the Labour Party see the catastrophe of Iraq, economic inequality and new school buildings laden with extractive PFI contracts, to name a few things that would be on the negative list. For some Labour members, these things can be acknowledged without coming to define New Labour. For others in and around the party, the size and seriousness of the mistakes has been difficult to look beyond. Then there is a deeper, cultural argument that I alluded to at the very beginning of this book. Tony Blair, Gordon Brown and the generation of politicians and staffers that worked with them remain in the British political consciousness in a way that other political generations (think John Major, David Cameron or even Margaret Thatcher) have not. New Labour is considered to be relevant, still, to today's times. When discussing the contemporary Labour Party, it is the go-to comparator, the source of many analogies – "it's their clause IV moment" – and the yardstick for political progress.

The historical debate has changed though. As academic historians continue to add detail and nuance to the New Labour story (see Murphy 2023a), a new generation of people in and around the Labour Party are forming their own opinions of New Labour. Someone turning 25 in 2024 was still in primary school when Tony Blair left Number 10. Younger political lives and memories have been made not with a Labour governing establishment but with a Conservative one. And there have been dramatic political events with ideology and the state of the nation at their centre: the global financial crisis, austerity and Brexit. These two things – works of academic history and the making of political lives in the context of our times – are very different. And I do not mean to suggest that the passage of time is rehabilitating New Labour by itself. Rather, what we grow to expect from our politics – and our assessment of the state of the nation at any one point in time – matters for how we view the performance and achievements of our politicians. Labour's public spending record, for example, was one thing, with David Cameron as a Conservative leader promising to safeguard public services prior to the global financial crisis. The Labour record looked rather different after a period of austerity and a decade of struggling public services. In short, it looked better.

This is all contributing to a reassessment of New Labour. It is not a writing out of the wrongs. But neither is it writing off New Labour as one big, missed opportunity. Such a context is, I think, a positive one for the Labour Party. Prior to becoming Keir Starmer's pollster, the public opinion expert Deborah Mattinson wrote a book on the Red Wall seats in England. She reported a sense, from voters, of Labour's working-class disconnect having begun with Blair: one of the many critical interpretations considered in this book. She also concluded that Labour needed a more politically healthy relationship with its recent past, writing (Mattinson 2020: 133): "While, of course, future electoral success will be contingent on Labour redefining itself for the future, it is hard to see how the party can overcome its deep-rooted negatives without some kind of rehabilitation of its most recent period in government and its most electorally successful leader ever."

This is not a simple process, and it isn't one that only involves people in and around the Labour Party. But it is a process that, perhaps, is beginning within Labour. Should Blair, and to a lesser extent Brown (because so much of the negativity is focused on the former), feel aggrieved that this political rehabilitation is necessary? After all, perhaps if Labour politicians had not chosen to heap criticism upon criticism on New Labour after 2010, the people of the United Kingdom may have had a more positive view both of New Labour and the party that followed it. I mostly reject this argument, for a couple of reasons.

The first reason is that, as Blair himself knows very well, politicians use history remorselessly to frame their present. As David Runciman wrote, Blair built his political reputation and projects "around his ability to embrace what is 'new'" (2006: 6). Indeed, Blair has continued doing this. New Labour replaced "old" Labour. At the turn of the century, everything was new. Globalization had brought great change and would continue to do so. When Blair really found his feet as prime minister, his domestic agenda was focused on reform. That meant insisting upon public services modernizing. Things could not stay the same, because the world had changed. Today, Blair heads the productive Tony Blair Institute for Global Change, and the message is much the same, with a hefty focus on technology and the resultant tech revolution. The relevant argument here is, what did Blair expect after he left office? If Blair's politics can be defined by his telling people that they must embrace the new, were his successors not entitled to do just the same?

The second reason is more focused on substance and the political art of emphasis, although it is connected to the above. In Chapter 1, I located Ed Miliband's critique of New Labour's political economy, and subsequently Jeremy Corbyn's same critique, within the inequality paradigm. Taking Thomas Piketty's analysis as an example of the power of this critique, I showed how both leaders criticized the New Labour project for its acquiescence within an economic system that created great reward for those at the top and persistent inequality. I also argued that, for Miliband, embracing this critique led to a dilemma. Other people in and around the Labour Party could say: "Yes, Ed, you are probably right about New Labour being too relaxed about inequality. But the focus was on poverty reduction, and that produced egalitarian outcomes. So, why do the Conservatives' work for them? Talk about inequality more, but don't whack New Labour over the head with it too often." Miliband's response to this, it seems to me, was to accept that New Labour did good things, but that his chosen (enhanced) emphasis was important to demonstrate that his approach was new.

It is on this specific point where the judgement of people in and around the Labour Party, after New Labour, is very much up for debate. It is possible that Miliband overcommitted in his criticisms of New Labour, particularly when his context – and chances of success – became very affected by the economic legacy of New Labour. From the Conservative Party came the criticism that New Labour had spent too much money and therefore, when the crash came, Britain was overexposed. From critics of the financialization of the British economy came the argument that New Labour had not done enough either to regulate financial services or to diversify the British economy so it was not too reliant on an industry that – through the global financial crisis – had demonstrated it could lead to calamity. Miliband bought into this second criticism, as well as adding the critique – analysed in Chapter 1 – of overseeing an economic system that accepted too much inequality. He then sought to rally around New Labour on the first criticism, about spending. Confused? You perhaps could not blame the public for being so.

There is one criticism of the Miliband years, and of the Corbyn project, that is relevant to the above argument, and one that I think is questionable: the suggestion that what replaced New Labour engaged in tactics that looked a lot like populism. For Diamond (2021: 333), Ed Miliband's leadership provided

> legitimacy for critics to attack the Blair/Brown legacy indiscriminately, defining the political territory of Corbynism. Miliband resorted to populist tropes subsequently deployed to lethal effect in the Corbyn era: the idea that politics is the virtuous battle of good versus evil; that the economy is controlled by sinister and predatory forces; that society has declined from the post-war golden age of social democracy to atomized individualism and selfishness under Thatcher and Blair.

This is similar to the argument from Clarke, discussed in the Introduction of this book, which considered "populism" on the British left to be constituted by three myths (2020: 29), similarly outlined by Diamond above. Populism, as I discussed in Chapter 2, means different things depending on how it is being understood as a political concept. In the more ideational sense, which I do not see as applying to the Labour Party, I agree with Müller that, in its construction of a "people", it is an exclusionary outlook and not pluralist (2017: 19–20). As a political strategy, which was the focus of Chapter 2 and the Corbyn project, the concept is interpreted in a different way and, as I noted, has its own problems. Regardless, the criticism of Miliband in particular appears to be focused on his critique of the economic system, and of New Labour's legacy.

It seems possible that some constructions within the inequality debate – specifically the 1 per cent and 99 per cent construction – could lend themselves to populist arguments about an "elite" pitched against a "people". Yet it does not automatically follow that to criticize wealth inequality in that way is to offer "populist tropes". For the contemporary socialist or social democrat, what Diamond and Clarke seem to pose is a quandary. If one accepts the analysis that, after a period where income and wealth inequality were partly constrained by social democracy (the "golden age" referred to above), and income from labour "predominated over inheritance" (Piketty 2017: 517), "patrimonial capitalism" (*ibid.*: 297) – where one inherits wealth – made a comeback, what do you do? As a socialist or social democrat, what do you say?

Presumably defending such inequalities is not an option for the socialist or social democrat. It becomes, then, a matter of language – and whether criticism of the political and economic relations of the time is justified, which it surely often is (Müller 2017: 2–3). How do you challenge such an economic system? The language of "predators" adopted by Miliband, or "rentiers" adopted by others today, may not be to everyone's particular political taste, but then the reality of people receiving large returns on capital – some of which is inherited – still exists. In relation to those with great wealth, Piketty wrote of the limits of the entrepreneurial defence, saying that "no matter how justified inequalities of wealth may be initially, fortunes can grow and perpetuate themselves beyond all reasonable limits and beyond any possible rational justification in terms of social utility" (2017: 561–2). To raise this is not class war, nor populism, but to debate our economic and social reality. On the Corbyn period and the misconception of populism, Maiguashca and Dean concluded much the same (2020: 59–60).

The touchstone

This takes me to the second, broad way we can address the question about getting over New Labour: New Labour as a touchstone. There is a risk that a more avowed attack on economic inequality be labelled "populist" because the politics of New Labour – and a rather ill-defined "centrism" – is seen as the only alternative to populism. Likewise, there is a danger that in seeking to move on from New Labour, political ideas and strategies associated with that project, or its leading figures, are rejected out-of-hand: "Blairite" is the usual term here. The booing of Tony Blair's name at Labour's 2011 conference – and the part he played, both directly and indirectly, during Corbyn's 2015 leadership triumph – epitomize his post-prime minister role as pantomime villain within the Labour Party. One need not be a huge Blair fan to see this as self-defeating. Jon Cruddas (2021: 148) wrote that Blair had been living in domestic political "exile":

Within Labour an enduring hostility ensures the party is unable to own its recent history, the victories and achievements, and aids political opponents who want the same. On leaving office politicians tend to be defined by their last defenders, usually those present at the political death. Often these are the most blinkered adherents of what the leader had become – rather than what they had once been or promised to be.

Cruddas identified something important when he noted that Blair's image today, and how New Labour has been reinterpreted, has contributed to its own toxicity. Liz Kendall, who ran in the 2015 Labour leadership contest, finishing last, recognized a short while afterwards that she had appeared to be "a little bit of the 'eat your greens' candidate ... that possibly wasn't the best way to win an internal leadership contest" (Stone 2016).

Kendall was undoubtedly right about that, and it speaks to what Cruddas was saying about the kind of touchstone New Labour became for people who believed they were acting in the tradition of New Labour. In reality, Blair the opposition politician was very different to how he has been interpreted and re-interpreted more recently (Pike & Hindmoor 2020). Returning to that moment during Ed Miliband's 2011 conference speech, what were people booing? They were not booing a particular mistake. They were booing what later became the reinterpretation of Blair, Blairism, neoliberalism and later New Labour, all of which became difficult to untangle. If the same people who had booed Blair were shown a video clip of Gordon Brown, in his last conference speech as prime minister, listing Labour's achievements in office (many of which were accomplished by Blair governments) – a moment that had the conference hall on its feet, clapping and cheering – I do not think they would boo. Blair, Brown, New Labour's achievements, the term "Blairite", New Labour's mistakes, these are all one and the same but simultaneously different. There is a "whole" there – and obviously an era – but one filled with contradictions. That's what makes using a political project, or a person, as a kind of touchstone a politically risky practice in contemporary politics. It doesn't encourage the disaggregation and nuance of the more complex historical debate I described above.

How has this kind of politics been self-defeating? Since 2010, there have been two very broad forms of using New Labour as a touchstone. The first – pro-New Labour – has focused mostly on electoral strategy and the route to victory. Owing to New Labour's three election victories, and the record of defeat after 1979, this version of New Labour as a touchstone sees criticism of the project, moves away from it on policy or different suggestions for electoral strategy as walking away from the voters New Labour – uniquely – brought together in its big tent. Clearly, there are lessons in Labour's past, including from the New Labour years, that provide some guidance as to how to win or lose votes. But with the touchstone approach, nuance is lost. Criticism of New Labour is seen – often by inference – as electorally calamitous, a sign that a person in and around the Labour Party is not serious about winning. This is, obviously, not a tenable political viewpoint. Even without relitigating the solidity of New Labour's electoral coalition towards the end of its time in office, nobody can credibly claim that there is one historical approach, relevant to contemporary politics, for putting together a winning electoral coalition in Britain.

The second touchstone is less about electoral strategy – although it does include it – and more about ideology. It is anti-New Labour, seeing even the project's achievements as limited, reversible and therefore suboptimal. The priority is distance from New Labour, seemingly above all else. Here, what politicians say is sometimes rapidly connected with New Labour, and therefore damned. When Keir Starmer is observed as moving away from Corbyn-era pledges, he is assumed to be "reconsolidating New Labourism with none of its original élan" (Eagleton 2022: 7). The anti-New Labour touchstone risks a much too simplistic analysis of the contemporary Labour Party and British politics more generally. It also risks too great an emphasis on rhetoric. There are Labour politicians who make very significant criticisms of New Labour central to their politics and political motivations (discussed below) yet offer a form of social democracy that, all too easily, is dismissed as vapidly New Labour-like (*ibid.*: 186). This form of analysis risks obscuring more than it reveals. And as a guide to public policy and decision-making, it is not always clear whether proximity or not to New Labour – across a whole host of policy areas – is all that relevant.

It is important to note, before moving to the final section of this chapter, how the two parts of getting over New Labour (past and touchstone) continue to be complicated by Blair himself. A version of "New Labour" and "Blairism" – highly flexible and permanently attached to Blair – is present in British politics through Blair's keen interest in public policy. The Tony Blair Institute for Global Change, mentioned earlier, was discussed by the *Financial Times* columnist Robert Shrimsley in 2023. "Tony Blair is not done with Britain", he wrote, suggesting that Blair's institute may well become the chief UK think tank and a source of ideas for an incoming Labour government. A restless Blair, keen to continue to push for reforms of Britain's public services, has a voice in the debate and could use it (Shrimsley 2023). Where does this leave the question of getting over New Labour, particularly treating New Labour as a kind of touchstone?

There is undoubtedly a risk that anything Blair says is affected by, and seen through, the prism of both the pro-New Labour touchstone of electoral genius and the anti-New Labour touchstone of ideological destruction. Both, in my view, should be resisted. The quality of the ideas produced by Blair's institute, like anything else, should be judged on their usefulness and applicability in today's political context. Similarly, if there is a danger for Starmer in adopting one of the touchstone views of New Labour, it is clearly the one about winning. So far, Starmer's relationship with this touchstone is rhetorical rather than substantive. As I discussed in Chapter 4, Starmer's ideology can be located within the tradition of labourism. His political strategy includes an emphasis on moving on from New Labour, particularly in the language of class. Saying that, a hesitancy remains. The winning-because-I-want-to-win argument, a tautological one, is quite possibly connected to the "serious politics" interpretation of New Labour. That takes us to the final concluding argument, explaining why New Labour will remain of political relevance for some time to come.

The "post-something" conjuncture

Whether it be reference to a new productivist paradigm, the end of globalization as we know it or debates about the ambition of modern supply-side economics, there is a sense that people are reaching for a "post-something", perhaps even a "post-neoliberalism" to use a phrase from the academic Todd Tucker (Meadway *et al.* 2023: 68). The one thing that all of these ideas do share is a post-1990s politics narrative. As the shadow chancellor Rachel Reeves wrote (2023: 42): "This marks a change from the wisdom of years gone by. The era of hyper-globalization, where an international free market reigned and nation states stood back, is dead. Policymakers must accept that, as they have done in the United States, Australia, Germany and many others."

Reeves noted that "globalization itself" was far from over, rather the way it needed to be understood and managed had changed. The end of globalization as we know it was also at the centre of Lisa Nandy's narrative about Labour, Britain and the policy choices of the future. In a particularly striking comment, Nandy wrote that after the political economic shocks of the 1980s, New Labour's election in 1997 "was the moment when, for so many of the casualties of globalization, the political route to a different future felt like it was closing" (2022: 42). Such a diagnosis is at the heart of an alternative approach for Labour, one that, in particular, seeks to decentralize power and develop parts of the United Kingdom that were perceived to have lost out through globalization.

As with the presidency of Bill Clinton in the United States, for British politics New Labour is the political centre of this story. I set out in Chapter 4 that the reasons for this "post" moment are many and contingent. In particular, a changing diplomatic and economic relationship with China is significant for the policy posture adopted in the United States. I do not wish to extensively replay the argument from Chapter 4 about what is absent from the Labour Party's ideology here. Suffice to say that President Biden's White House has opted to talk about taxing wealth, noting that "for too long, our tax code has rewarded wealth, not work, and contributed to growing income and wealth inequality in America" (White House 2022). Without action on tax, and without significant redistribution, I do not think Labour's ambitions for a more equal society, and for correcting some of the economic problems that have been features of the UK economy since the 1980s, can be realized. In a sense, this returns us to the ongoing significance of New Labour and why the project will still be debated.

Starmer's Labour – partly owing to the influence of Bidenomics, partly owing to the longer-running narrative of globalization and its effects – has within its political economy some clear "moving on from New Labour" thinking. Globalization was central to Blair's approach: it was a source of the new, it mandated the new, it was the politics that you could not avoid. Today, a very different reading of globalization is stimulating new economic ideas. Yet it is still possible that some of the vague interpretations attached to New Labour about electoral success, and being careful about what you commit to and what you say, are also acting to hold back the "moving on" part of Labour's approach. As the Labour MP Stella Creasy put it (2022): "As many still obsess about New Labour, it risks becoming the political equivalent of *Friends*: endlessly replayed as new generations pick apart what was right and wrong while failing to produce new ideas."

If the Labour Party exits opposition and enters power, things may be different. Politicians in office feel they can more easily affect the political weather, and their impact is judged very differently. In other words, some of the hesitation within Labour may fall away. If it does not – either in office or in continued opposition – Labour may well be facing the future but still be partly hamstrung by its past.

REFERENCES

Allen, P. 2018. *The Political Class*. Oxford: Oxford University Press.

Allen, P. & D. Moon 2020. "Predictions, pollification, and pol profs: the 'Corbyn problem' beyond Corbyn". *Political Quarterly* 91(1): 80–88.

Anderson, E. 2017. *Private Government*. Princeton, NJ: Princeton University Press.

Asthana, A. 2016. "Labour in for Britain chair criticised Jeremy Corbyn's campaign involvement". *The Guardian*, 26 June. https://www.theguardian.com/politics/2016/jun/26/corbyn-labour-in-for-britain-chair-phil-wilson-eu-referendum.

Asthana, A. & J. Elgot 2016. "Owen Smith to face Corbyn in Labour leadership challenge". *The Guardian*, 19 July. https://www.theguardian.com/politics/2016/jul/19/owen-smith-jeremy-corbyn-labour-leadership-angela-eagle.

Asthana, A., R. Syal & J. Elgot 2016. "Labour MPs prepare for leadership contest after Corbyn loses confidence vote". *The Guardian*, 28 June. https://www.theguardian.com/politics/2016/jun/28/jeremy-corbyn-loses-labour-mps-confidence-vote.

Atkinson, A. 2015. *Inequality*. Cambridge, MA: Harvard University Press.

Attlee, C. 1937. *The Labour Party in Perspective*. London: Victor Gollancz.

Avril, E. 2019. "The 'movementisation' of the Labour Party and the future of labour organising". In E. Avril & Y. Beliard (eds), *Labour United and Divided from the 1830s to the Present*, 254–70. Manchester: Manchester University Press.

Bale, T. 2012. *The Conservatives since 1945*. Oxford: Oxford University Press.

Bale, T. 2015. *Five Year Mission*. Oxford: Oxford University Press.

Bale, T. 2023. *The Conservative Party after Brexit*. Cambridge: Polity.

Bale, T., P. Webb & M. Poletti 2020. *Footsoldiers*. Abingdon: Routledge.

Batty, D. 2010. "David Miliband: time to move on from Iraq". *The Guardian*, 22 May. https://www.theguardian.com/politics/2010/may/22/david-miliband-iraq-war-labour-leadership.

BBC News 2015. "Jeremy Corbyn makes his pitch for Labour Leadership – BBC Newsnight". BBC, 8 June. https://www.youtube.com/watch?v=q-gJD6PvUO0.

BBC News 2020. "Black Lives Matter: Sir Keir Starmer 'regrets' calling movement a 'moment'". BBC News, 2 July. https://www.bbc.co.uk/news/uk-politics-53267989.

BBC News 2023a. "No plans to increase capital gains tax, Labour says". BBC News, 30 March. https://www.bbc.co.uk/news/uk-politics-65122284.

BBC News 2023b. "Labour splits row reignited – BBC Newsnight". BBC, 4 July. https://www.bbc.co.uk/iplayer/episode/m001nk48/newsnight-labour-splits-row-reignited.

Beckett, A. 2023. "Starmer may lack Blair's charisma, but he may well change Britain more than New Labour ever did". *The Guardian*, 6 January. https://www.theguardian.com/commentisfree/2023/jan/06/keir-starmer-tony-blair-reform-new-labour-90s.

Behr, R. 2011. "Ed Miliband might have read too much into phone-hacking". *New Statesman*, 10 November. https://www.newstatesman.com/politics/2011/11/phone-hacking-labour-miliband.

BEIS (Department for Business, Energy & Industrial Strategy) 2022. *Trade Union Membership, UK 1995–2021: Statistical Bulletin*. London: BEIS.

Bell, T. *et al.* 2023. *We're Going on a Growth Hunt: Putting the 2023 Spring Budget in Context*. London: Resolution Foundation.

Berman, S. & M. Snegovaya 2019. "Populism and the decline of social democracy". *Journal of Democracy* 30(3): 5–19.

Berry, C. & J. Guinan 2019. *People Get Ready!* London: OR Books.

Bevir, M. 2011. *The Making of British Socialism*. Princeton, NJ: Princeton University Press.

Bevir, M. & J. Blakely 2018. *Interpretive Social Science*. Oxford: Oxford University Press.

Blair, T. 2011. "Foreword". In P. Gould, *The Unfinished Revolution*, ix–xxvi. London: Abacus.

Blair, T. 2013. "Tony Blair: Labour must search for answers and not merely aspire to be a repository for people's anger". *New Statesman*, 11 April. https://www.newstatesman.com/politics/2013/04/labour-must-search-answers-and-not-merely-aspire-be-repository-peoples-anger.

Blair, T. 2015. "Tony Blair: even if you hate me, please don't take Labour over the cliff edge". *The Guardian*, 13 August. https://www.theguardian.com/commentisfree/2015/aug/12/even-if-hate-me-dont-take-labour-over-cliff-edge-tony-blair.

Blakeley, G. 2021. "Public spending isn't socialism". *Tribune*, 8 November. https://tribunemag.co.uk/2021/10/public-spending-isnt-socialism/.

Blunkett, D. 2023. "My party is better than this brand of gutter politics, writes former Labour Home Secretary David Blunkett". *Daily Mail*, 7 April. https://www.dailymail.co.uk/news/article-11950721/An-absolute-shocker-Labours-hardliners-hate-attack-ad.html.

Boffey, D. 2011. "How the fish market porters moved Ed Miliband in his search to rekindle Labour's flame". *The Observer*, 24 April. https://www.theguardian.com/politics/2011/apr/24/miliband-billingsgate-blue-labour.

Bolton, M. & F. Pitts 2018. *Corbynism: A Critical Approach*. Bingley: Emerald.

Booth, R. 2015. "Jeremy Corbyn's Labour leadership bid gathers pace as supporters flock to rally". *The Guardian*, 3 August. https://www.theguardian.com/politics/2015/aug/03/jeremy-corbyn-bid-labour-leadership-momentum-supporters-flock-london-rally.

Brown, G. 2017. *My Life, Our Times*. London: Bodley Head.

Brown, J. 2019. "London's famous fish market is leaving town, taking hundreds of years of tradition with it". *Prospect*, 5 October. https://www.prospectmagazine.co.uk/magazine/londons-famous-fish-market-is-leaving-town-taking-hundreds-of-years-of-tradition-with-it-billingsgate.

Brown, M. & R. Jones 2021. *Paint Your Town Red*. London: Repeater Books.

Brusseler, M. 2023. *Coordinating the Green Prosperity Plan*. 15 June. https://www.common-wealth.co.uk/publications/coordinating-the-green-prosperity-plan#top.

Burton, M. & R. Tunnicliffe 2022. *Membership of Political Parties in Great Britain*. House of Commons Library. https://researchbriefings.files.parliament.uk/documents/SN 05125/SN05125.pdf.

Butt, S., E. Clery & J. Curtice (eds) 2022. "Taxation, welfare and inequality". *British Social Attitudes: The 39th Report*. London: National Centre for Social Research. https://www.bsa.natcen.ac.uk/media/39481/bsa39_taxation-welfare-and-inequality.pdf.

Calhoun, C. 2022. "Contradictions and double movements". In C. Calhoun, D. Gaonkar & C. Taylor (eds), *Degenerations of Democracy*, 48–87. Cambridge, MA: Harvard University Press.

Cameron, D. 2010. "David Cameron's speech outside 10 Downing Street as Prime Minister". Gov.uk, 11 May. https://www.gov.uk/government/speeches/david-camerons-speech-outside-10-downing-street-as-prime-minister.

Campbell, A. 2017. *From Blair to Brown – Diaries: Volume 6, 2005–2007*. London: Biteback.

Campbell, A. 2018a. "Ed Miliband has reasons to be cheerful". *GQ*, 24 April. https://www.gq-magazine.co.uk/article/ed-miliband-interview.

Campbell, A. 2018b. *From Crash to Defeat – Diaries: Volume 7, 2007–2010*. London: Biteback.

Campbell, A. 2021. *Rise and Fall of the Olympic Spirit – Diaries: Volume 8, 2010–2015*. London: Biteback.

Canovan, M. 1995. *Hannah Arendt: A Reinterpretation of Her Political Thought*. Cambridge: Cambridge University Press.

Chakrabortty, A. 2023. "Suella Braverman proved it again: racism is a fire the Tories love to play with". *The Guardian*, 19 January. https://www.theguardian.com/commentis free/2023/jan/19/suella-braverman-racism-tories-holocaust.

Cheng-Morris, J. 2021. "'Lose, lose, lose, lose Blair, Blair, Blair, lose, lose, lose, lose': 11 words that sum up Labour's problem". Yahoo! News, 7 May. https://uk.news.yahoo.com/blunt-message-labour-hartlepool-defeat-100943383.html.

Chessum, M. 2022. *This Is Only the Beginning: The Making of a New Left, From Anti-Austerity to the Fall of Corbyn*. London: Bloomsbury Academic.

Chesterton, G. 2020. "Alan Johnson: 'part of Labour's far left despises working class culture'". *GQ*, 3 December. https://www.gq-magazine.co.uk/politics/article/alan-johnson-interview.

Clarke, C. 2020. *The Dark Knight and the Puppet Master*. London: Penguin.

Cohen, G. 2009. *Why Not Socialism?* Princeton, NJ: Princeton University Press.

Corbyn, J. 2015a. "Labour should be more aspirational – about closing the huge inequality gap". *The Guardian*, 8 June. https://www.theguardian.com/commentisfree/2015/jun/08/labour-leadership.

Corbyn, J. 2015b. "Jeremy Corbyn". In A. Burnham *et al.* (eds), *Leading Labour*, 14–16. London: Fabian Society.

Corbyn, J. 2015c. Speech to 2015 Labour Party Annual Conference. http://www.british politicalspeech.org/speech-archive.htm?speech=359.

Corbyn, J. 2016. Speech to 2016 Labour Party Annual Conference. http://www. britishpoliticalspeech.org/speech-archive.htm?speech=363.

Corbyn, J. 2018. "Labour is back as the political voice of the working class – Corbyn". Labour Party press release, 3 July. https://labour.org.uk/press/labour-back-political-voice-working-class-corbyn/.

Corbyn, J. 2019. "Jeremy Corbyn's Brexit speech in Harlow". 5 November. https://labour. org.uk/press/jeremy-corbyns-brexit-speech-in-harlow/.

Corbyn, J. 2020. "Jeremy Corbyn: 'we didn't go far enough'". Interview with R. Burtenshaw, *Tribune*, 11 October. https://tribunemag.co.uk/2020/10/jeremy-corbyn-we-didnt-go-far-enough.

Corlett, A. 2019. *The Shifting Shape of UK Tax: Charting the Changing Size and Shape of the UK Tax System*. London: Resolution Foundation.

Corlett, A. 2023. *Happy New Tax Year 2023!* London: Resolution Foundation.

Cowley, P. & D. Kavanagh 2016. *The British General Election of 2015*. Basingstoke: Palgrave Macmillan.

Cowley, P. & D. Kavanagh 2018. *The British General Election of 2017*. Basingstoke: Palgrave Macmillan.

Crace, J. 2017. "The making of the Maybot: a year of mindless slogans, U-turns and denials". *The Guardian*, 10 July. https://www.theguardian.com/politics/2017/jul/10/making-maybot-theresa-may-rise-and-fall.

Creasy, S. 2022. "New Labour risks becoming like Friends: endlessly repeated without new ideas". *The Independent*, 10 May. https://www.independent.co.uk/voices/new-labour-tony-blair-25-years-b2075509.html.

Creasy, S. 2023. "Beyond referendums and recriminations: rebuilding the UK's relationship with the EU". *Renewal* 31(2): 24–32.

Creasy, S. & K. Pike 2021. "Nothing is inevitable: narrating the Covid crisis". *Renewal* 21(1): 38–48.

Crerar, P. 2022. "Keir Starmer rules out return of free movement between Britain and EU". *The Guardian*, 27 November. https://www.theguardian.com/politics/2022/nov/27/keir-starmer-rules-out-return-free-movement-britain-eu.

Cruddas, J. 2021. *The Dignity of Labour*. Cambridge: Polity.

Dathan, M. 2023. "Labour will blame PM for crashing economy; controversial attack ads to go on, vows party". *The Times*, 10 April.

Davis, J. & J. Rentoul 2019. *Heroes or Villains?* Oxford: Oxford University Press.

Demianyk, G. 2015. "Jeremy Corbyn voted against welfare bill because it was 'rotten and indefensible'". *Huffington Post*, 22 July. https://www.huffingtonpost.co.uk/2015/07/22/jeremy-corbyn-welfare-bill-labour-leader_n_7849434.html.

Dewey, J. 2008a. *The Middle Works, 1899–1924: Volume 9 1916*. Carbondale: Southern Illinois University Press.

Dewey, J. 2008b. *The Later Works, 1925–1953: Volume 2 1925–1927*. Carbondale: Southern Illinois University Press.

Diamond, P. 2016. *The Crosland Legacy*. Bristol: Policy Press.

Diamond, P. 2021. *The British Labour Party in Opposition and Power 1979–2019*. London: Routledge.

Dickson, A. & E. Webber 2023. "Keir Starmer wants to be UK prime minister: now he needs ideas for government". *Politico*, 23 February. https://www.politico.eu/article/keir-starmer-uk-labour-policy-election-ideology/.

Dorey, P. & A. Denham 2016. "Entirely as expected? What the voting data tells us about Corbyn's re-election". LSE British Politics and Policy Blog, 26 September. https://blogs.lse.ac.uk/politicsandpolicy/labour-2016-voting-data/.

Driver, S. & L. Martell 2006. *New Labour*. Cambridge: Polity.

Drucker, H. 1979. *Doctrine and Ethos in the Labour Party*. London: Allen & Unwin.

Duncan, P. 2021. "Treasury could raise £16bn a year if shares and property were taxed like salaries". *The Guardian*, 26 October. https://www.theguardian.com/politics/2021/oct/26/uk-shares-property-capital-gains-tax.

Eagleton, O. 2022. *The Starmer Project*. London: Verso.

EHRC (Equality and Human Rights Commission) 2020. *Investigation into Antisemitism in the Labour Party, Report October 2020*. https://www.equalityhumanrights.com/sites/default/files/investigation-into-antisemitism-in-the-labour-party.pdf.

EHRC (Equality and Human Rights Commission) 2023. "Equality watchdog concludes monitoring of Labour Party action plan". News, 15 February. https://equalityhumanrights.com/en/our-work/news/equality-watchdog-concludes-monitoring-labour-party-action-plan.

Elgot, J. 2022a. "Shadow ministers question Labour's stance on strikes after Tarry sacking". *The Guardian*, 27 July. https://www.theguardian.com/politics/2022/jul/27/sam-tarry-sacked-labour-frontbench-rail-strike-picket-line-keir-starmer.

Elgot, J. 2022b. "Labour facing 'breakdown in discipline' as Nandy visits picket line". *The Guardian*, 1 August. https://www.theguardian.com/politics/2022/aug/01/bt-and-openreach-strike-lisa-nandy-visits-picket-line-in-wigan.

Elgot, J. 2022c. "Starmer takes aim at loose cannons with his tight control of Labour selections". *The Guardian*, 13 November. https://www.theguardian.com/politics/2022/nov/13/starmer-takes-aim-loose-cannons-tight-control-labour-selections.

Elgot, J. & M. Taylor 2015. "Calais crisis: Cameron condemned for 'dehumanising' description of migrants". *The Guardian*, 30 July. https://www.theguardian.com/uk-news/2015/jul/30/david-cameron-migrant-swarm-language-condemned.

Elliot, L. 2013. "George Osborne told by IMH chief: rethink your austerity plan". *The Guardian*, 18 April. https://www.theguardian.com/politics/2013/apr/18/george-osborne-imf-austerity.

Elliot, L. 2021. "IMF calls for wealth tax to help cover cost of Covid pandemic". *The Guardian*, 7 April. https://www.theguardian.com/business/2021/apr/07/imf-wealth-tax-cost-covid-pandemic-rich-poor. Errejón, I. & C. Mouffe 2016. *Podemos: In the Name of the People*. London: Lawrence & Wishart.

Esping-Andersen, G. 1985. *Politics against Markets*. Princeton, NJ: Princeton University Press.

Evans, G. & J. Tilley 2017. *The New Politics of Class*. Oxford: Oxford University Press.

FBU 2015. "FBU in historic affiliation to Labour". FBU.org.uk, 30 November. https://www.fbu.org.uk/news/2015/11/30/fbu-historic-affiliation-labour.

Ferguson, M. 2013. "Ed Miliband interview: part two – on selections, community organising and the future of the Labour Party". LabourList, 1 April. https://labourlist.org/2013/04/ed-miliband-interview-part-two-on-selections-community-organising-and-the-future-of-the-labour-party/.

Finlayson, A. 2003. *Making Sense of New Labour*. London: Lawrence & Wishart.Freeden, M. 1996. *Ideologies and Political Theory*. Oxford: Oxford University Press.

Gamble, A. 2021. *The Western Ideology and Other Essays*. Bristol: Bristol University Press.

Ganesh, J. 2014. *George Osborne*. London: Biteback.

Ganesh, J. 2023. "Starmer's war on the left is unfinished". *Financial Times*, 11 April. https://www.ft.com/content/3e7a2cab-d893-444c-8e65-ad542c58627f.

Garland, N. & K. Pike 2023. "Editorial: facing the problems". *Renewal* 31(2): 7–15.

Gayle, D. 2015. "Labour MP Jeremy Corbyn to run for leadership on anti-austerity platform". *The Guardian*, 4 June. https://www.theguardian.com/politics/2015/jun/04/labour-mp-jeremy-corbyn-leadership-anti-austerity-platform.

Geuss, R. 2001. *History and Illusion in Politics*. Cambridge: Cambridge University Press.

Geuss, R. 2008. *Philosophy and Real Politics*. Princeton, NJ: Princeton: University Press.

Geuss, R. 2020. *Who Needs a World View?* Cambridge, MA: Harvard University Press.

Glasman, M. 2022. *Blue Labour*. Cambridge: Polity.

Glasman, M. *et al.* (eds) 2011. *The Labour Tradition and the Politics of Paradox*. The Oxford London Seminars 2010–11. https://static1.squarespace.com/static/5d1890f32eb7e50001d7bb7f/t/6292447f74726d213fe76114/1653752961593/Labour_tradition_and_the_politics_of_paradox.pdf

Goes, E. 2016. *The Labour Party under Ed Miliband*. Manchester: Manchester University Press.

Goes, E. 2021. "Ideas and party change: the role of predistribution in Labour's ideological renewal". *Journal of Political Ideologies* 26(2): 180–200.

Goldhammer, A. 2017. "The Piketty phenomenon". In H. Boushey, J. Delong & M. Steinbaum (eds), *After Piketty*, 27–47. Cambridge, MA: Harvard University Press.

Gould, P. 2011. *The Unfinished Revolution: How New Labour Changed British Politics Forever*. London: Abacus.

Graf, A. 2020. *Lessons Learned*. Chicago: ACTA.

Grylls, G. 2022. "Starmer ally Wes Streeting apologises after backing union over rail strikes". *The Times*, 16 July.

Guinan, J. & M. O'Neill 2018. "Editorial – the new institutional turn: Labour's new political economy". *Renewal* 26(2): 5–16.

Hall, S. 2017. *Selected Political Writings*. Durham, NC: Duke University Press.

Hansard HC Deb (20 July 2015), Vol. 598, col. 1315.

Hansard HC Deb (29 June 2016), Vol. 612, col. 294.

Hansard HC Deb (31 October 2022), Vol. 721, col. 641.

Hansard HC Deb (24 May 2023), Vol. 733, col. 282.

Harman, H. 2015. Interview on BBC Sunday Politics, 12 July. https://www.bbc.co.uk/news/av/uk-politics-33498738.

Harman, H. 2017. *A Woman's Work*. London: Allen Lane.

Hasan, M. & J. Macintyre 2012. *Ed: The Milibands and the Making of a Labour Leader*. London: Biteback.

Hattenstone, S. 2019. "Tom Watson: 'Was I disloyal? I don't take kindly to being told what to do'". *The Guardian*, 28 December. https://www.theguardian.com/politics/2019/dec/28/tom-watson-was-i-disloyal-i-dont-take-kindly-to-being-told-what-to-do.

Hay, C. 1999. *The Political Economy of New Labour*. Manchester: Manchester University Press.

Hay, C. 2002. *Political Analysis*. Basingstoke: Palgrave.

Heffernan, R. 2000. *New Labour and Thatcherism: Political Change in Britain*. Basingstoke: Macmillan.

Helm, T. 2011. "Rupert Murdoch's only the start, the psyche of British politics has changed". *The Observer*, 16 July. https://www.theguardian.com/politics/2011/jul/16/ed-miliband-rupert-murdoch-phone-hacking.

Helm, T. 2012. "Ed Miiband to wage war on George Osborne over benefit cuts". *The Observer*, 9 December. https://www.theguardian.com/politics/2012/dec/08/ed-miliband-george-osborne-welfare.

Helm, T. 2018. "McDonnell: Labour will give power to workers through 'ownership funds'". *The Observer*, 8 September. https://www.theguardian.com/politics/2018/sep/08/john-mcdonnell-labour-proposal-workers-ownership-funds.

Hindmoor, A. 2004. *New Labour at the Centre*. Oxford: Oxford University Press.

Hindmoor, A. & K. Pike 2022. "Past, present and future: Tony Blair and the political legacy of New Labour". In N. Yeowell (ed.), *Rethinking Labour's Past*, 249–65. London: I. B. Tauris.

Hobsbawm, E. 1989. *Politics for a Rational Left*. London: Verso.

Hobsbawm, E. 2012. *How to Change the World*. London: Abacus.

Honneth, A. 2017. *The Idea of Socialism*. Cambridge: Polity.

Hunsaker, S. 2023. "What Sunak's tax return tells us about the UK tax system". UK in a Changing Europe, 18 April. https://ukandeu.ac.uk/what-sunaks-tax-return-tells-us-about-the-uk-tax-system/.

IFS TaxLab 2021. "How have government revenues changed over time?" Institute for Fiscal Studies. https://ifs.org.uk/taxlab/taxlab-key-questions/how-have-government-revenues-changed-over-time.

Institute for Fiscal Studies 2015. "Press release: public finance plans for Conservatives, Labour, Liberal Democrats and SNP leave much unanswered". London: IFS. https://ifs.org.uk/uploads/publications/pr/PostElectionAusterityPR.pdf.

IPPR 2021. "Labour's £28 billion investment pledge to achieve net zero is 'welcome recognition' of scale of challenge, says IPPR". IPPR, 27 September. https://www.ippr.org/news-and-media/press-releases/labour-s-28-billion-investment-pledge-to-achieve-net-zero-is-welcome-recognition-of-scale-of-challenge-says-ippr.

Jackson, B. 2007. *Equality and the British Left*. Manchester: Manchester University Press.

Jackson, B. 2017. "The politics of the Labour manifesto". *Political Quarterly* 88(3): 343–4.

Jackson, B. 2018. "Learning from New Labour". *Political Quarterly* 89(1): 3–4.

Jackson, B. 2022. "What we talk about when we talk about the Labour Party". *Political Quarterly* 93(3): 381–2.

Jäger, A. 2023. "Everything is hyperpolitical". *The Point*, 22 February. https://thepointmag.com/politics/everything-is-hyperpolitical/.

Jones, O. 2015. "Jeremy Corbyn is in the Labour leadership race: the real debate starts here". *The Guardian*, 4 June. https://www.theguardian.com/commentisfree/2015/jun/04/jeremy-corbyn-vital-labour-leadership-debate.

Jones, O. 2017. "New Labour is dead: Jeremy Corbyn's shadow cabinet must stay as it is". *The Guardian*, 13 June. https://www.theguardian.com/commentisfree/2017/jun/13/new-labour-dead-jeremy-corbyn-shadow-cabinet-socialist-labour.

Jones, O. 2019. "'Soft' Brexit is dead: now Labour must really embrace a people's vote". *The Guardian*, 27 June. https://www.theguardian.com/commentisfree/2019/jun/27/soft-brexit-dead-labour-peoples-vote-referendum-remain.

Jones, O. 2020. *This Land: The Story of a Movement*. London: Allen Lane.

Jones, S. 2005. "Heckler, 82, wins apology from Labour". *The Guardian*, 29 September. https://www.theguardian.com/politics/2005/sep/29/uk.labourconference.

Jordan, W. 2015. "Health overtakes immigration as an issue for voters". YouGov, 15 April. https://yougov.co.uk/topics/politics/articles-reports/2015/04/15/health-tops-immigration-second-most-important-issu.

Kale, S. 2020. "Keir Starmer: 'I still see myself as a socialist'". *Vice*, 17 March. https://www.vice.com/en/article/pkev7y/keir-starmer-i-still-see-myself-as-a-socialist.

Kennedy, S., R. Cracknell & R. McInnes 2013. "Welfare Benefits Uprating Bill: Research Paper 13/01". London: House of Commons Library.

Kentish, B. 2019. "'The abuse made me physically ill': Luciana Berger reveals toll of fighting antisemitism while Labour MPs refused to stand by her". *The Independent*, 9 November. https://www.independent.co.uk/news/uk/politics/luciana-berger-labour-antisemitism-jeremy-corbyn-election-latest-liberal-democrats-finchley-a9196696.html.

Klug, A., E. Rees & J. Schneider 2016. "Momentum: a new kind of politics". *Renewal* 24(2): 36–44.

Kogan, D. 2019. *Protest and Power*. London: Bloomsbury.

Labour Party 2015. *Britain Can Be Better*. London: Labour Party.

Labour Party 2017a. *For the Many Not the Few*. London: Labour Party.

Labour Party 2017b. *Funding Britain's Future*. London: Labour Party.

Labour Party 2019a. *It's Time for Real Change*. London: Labour Party.

Labour Party 2019b. *Funding Real Change*. London: Labour Party.

Labour Party 2022a. *Prosperity through Partnership*. London: Labour Party.

Labour Party 2022b. *Employment Rights Green Paper: A New Deal for Working People*. London: Labour Party.

Labour Party 2022c. *A New Britain: Renewing Our Democracy and Rebuilding Our Economy – a Report of the Commission on the UK's Future*. London: Labour Party.

Labour Party 2023a. *A "Mission-Driven" Government to End "Sticking Plaster" Politics*. London: Labour Party.

Labour Party 2023b. "Labour is the party of law and order". Twitter, 6 April. https://twitter.com/UKLabour/status/1643973886311297028.

Labour Party 2023c. *Make Britain a Clean Energy Superpower*. London: Labour Party.

Labour Party 2023d. *Breaking down the Barriers to Opportunity*. London: Labour Party.

Laclau, E. 2018. *On Populist Reason*. London: Verso.

Larik, J., J. Harkonen & S. Hix 2022. "Will support for Brexit become extinct?" UK in a Changing Europe, 30 November. https://ukandeu.ac.uk/will-support-for-brexit-become-extinct/.

Lawder, D. & A. Shalal 2022. "Yellen rebrands Biden economic agenda as 'modern supply-side economics'". Reuters, 21 January. https://www.reuters.com/business/yellen-rebrands-biden-economic-agenda-modern-supply-side-economics-2022-01-21/.

Lawrence, J. 2020. "Vernacular social democracy and the politics of Labour". *Renewal* 28(3): 38–42.

Lukes, S. 2021. *Power: A Radical View*, 3rd edition. London: Red Globe Press.

Lynch, M. 2022. "An interview with Mick Lynch". Interview with R. Burtenshaw, *Tribune* 16: 7–11.

Maccaferri, M. 2021. "How Gramsci went global". *Tribune*, 30 October. https://tribunemag.co.uk/2021/10/how-gramsci-went-global.

Macintyre, J. 2010. "Brothers at arms". *New Statesman*, 17 June. https://www.newstatesman.com/long-reads/2010/06/david-miliband-labour.

Maiguashca, B. & J. Dean 2020. "'Lovely people but utterly deluded?'" *British Politics* 15: 48–68.

Mair, P. 2013. *Ruling the Void*. London: Verso.

Mandelson, P. 2015. *Andrew Marr Show* interview transcript, 10 May. http://news.bbc.co.uk/1/shared/bsp/hi/pdfs/10_05_15_lord_mandelson.pdf.

Manwaring, R., G. Duncan & C. Lees 2023. "'Thin labourism': ideological and policy comparisons between the Australian, British, and New Zealand labour parties". *British Journal of Politics and International Relations.* https://doi.org/10.1177/13691481221148326.

Marquand, D. 1999. *The Progressive Dilemma: From Lloyd George to Blair*, 2nd edition. London: Phoenix.

Marr, A. 2023. "How Labour lost the moral high ground". *New Statesman*, 12 April. https://www.newstatesman.com/politics/uk-politics/2023/04/labour-lost-moral-high-ground-rishi-sunak-attack-ads.

Mason, R. 2019. "Labour's Brexit position set MPs up to fail, says Lisa Nandy". *The Guardian*, 20 December. https://www.theguardian.com/politics/2019/dec/20/labours-brexit-position-set-mps-up-to-fail-says-lisa-nandy.

Mattinson, D. 2020. *Beyond the Red Wall*. London: Biteback.

Mazzucato, M. 2021. *Mission Economy*. London: Allen Lane.

Mazzucato, M. 2023. "To succeed, Keir Starmer needs to be much more than 'business friendly'". *New Statesman*, 3 March. https://www.newstatesman.com/comment/2023/03/succeed-keir-starmer-needs-business-friendly.

McDonnell, J. 2012. "An open letter to fellow Labour MPs from John McDonnell". Labour List, 6 December. https://labourlist.org/2012/12/an-open-letter-to-fellow-labour-mps-from-john-mcdonnell/.

McDonnell, J. 2016. Speech to 2016 Labour Party Annual Conference. https://www.policyforum.labour.org.uk/news/john-mcdonnell-s-speech-to-annual-conference-2016.

McDonnell, J. 2018a. "Introduction". In J. McDonnell (ed.), *Economics for the Many*, vi–xviii. London: Verso.

McDonnell, J. 2018b. Lecture on Economic Policy of the Labour Party to Marx Memorial Library. https://vimeo.com/293440778.

McDonnell, J. 2018c. Speech to 2018 Labour Party Annual Conference. https://labour.org.uk/press/john-mcdonnells-full-speech-labour-conference-2018/.

McDonnell, J. 2021. "Interview with John McDonnell by Seth Wheeler". In S. Wheeler & London Edinburgh Weekend Return Group (eds), *In and Against the State*, 135–50. London: Pluto.

McDonnell, J. 2023. "This is not the sort of politics … ". Twitter, 6 April. https://twitter.com/johnmcdonnellMP/status/1644066942867894272.

Meadway, J. 2020. "Finance and left strategy". In G. Blakeley (ed.), *Futures of Socialism*, 158–65. London: Verso.

Meadway, J., C. Roberts & T. Tucker 2023. "Modern supply-side: the centre left's new economic agenda?" *Renewal* 31(2): 58–70.

Merrick, J. 2013. "Arnie Graf: the sage who can see Ed Miliband at No. 10". *The Independent*, 10 November. https://www.independent.co.uk/news/people/profiles/arnie-graf-the-sage-who-can-see-ed-miliband-at-no-10-8930921.html.

Midgley, M. 1983. *Heart and Mind: The Varieties of Moral Experience*. Abingdon: Routledge.

Midgley, M. 2000. *Utopias, Dolphins and Computers: Problems of Philosophical Plumbing*. London: Routledge.

Midgley, M. 2011. *The Myths We Live by*. Abingdon: Routledge.

Milburn, K. 2019. *Generation Left*. Cambridge: Polity.

Miliband, D. 2008. "Against all odds we can still win, on a platform for change". *The Guardian*, 29 July. https://www.theguardian.com/commentisfree/2008/jul/29/davidmiliband.labour.

Miliband, D. 2010. "David Miliband". In D. Abbott *et al.*, *The Labour Leadership*. London: Fabian Society. https://fabians.org.uk/wp-content/uploads/2010/08/TheLabourLeadership.pdf.

Miliband, D. 2017. *Rescue: Refugees and the Political Crisis of Our Time*. London: TED BOOKS/Simon & Schuster.

Miliband, E. 2006. "Why ideology matters". Speech to Fabian Society Northern Conference, "The Next Future of Socialism", 16 September. https://web.archive.org/web/20070520033132/http://www.fabian-society.org.uk/documents/ViewADocument.asp?ID=142&CatID=52.

Miliband, E. 2007. "Renewing the domestic agenda". In N. Pearce & J. Margo (eds), *Politics for a New Generation: The Progressive Moment*, 29–40. Basingstoke: Palgrave Macmillan.

Miliband, E. 2010a. "Why I want to lead the Labour party". *The Guardian*, 15 May. https://www.theguardian.com/commentisfree/2010/may/15/ed-miliband-labour-leadership.

Miliband, E. 2010b. "Ed Miliband". In D. Abbott *et al.*, *The Labour Leadership*, 55–66. London: The Fabian Society.

Miliband, E. 2010c. Speech to 2010 Labour Party Conference. http://www.british politicalspeech.org/speech-archive.htm?speech=212.

Miliband, E. 2011a. "Speech to the Fabians". https://www.newstatesman.com/politics/2011/01/labour-government-politics.

Miliband, E. 2011b. "Ed Miliband: business, finance and politics are out of touch with people". *The Guardian*, 6 November. https://www.theguardian.com/commentis free/2011/nov/05/ed-miliband-business-finance-politics.

Miliband, E. 2011c. Speech to 2011 Labour Party Annual Conference. http://www.britishpoliticalspeech.org/speech-archive.htm?speech=312.

Miliband, E. 2012. Speech to 2012 Labour Party Annual Conference. http://www.britishpoliticalspeech.org/speech-archive.htm?speech=323.

Miliband, E. 2013a. Speech on Labour and the trade unions. https://labourlist.org/2013/07/ed-miliband-speech-on-the-union-link-full-text/.

Miliband, E. 2013b. Speech to 2013 Labour Party Annual Conference. http://www.britishpoliticalspeech.org/speech-archive.htm?speech=353.

Miliband, E. 2014a. "The Choice of Leadership". LabourList, 25 July. https://labourlist.org/2014/07/the-choice-of-leadership-read-the-full-text-of-ed-milibands-speech/.

Miliband, E. 2014b. Speech to 2014 Labour Party Annual Conference. http://www.britishpoliticalspeech.org/speech-archive.htm?speech=355.

Miliband, E. 2016. "The inequality problem". *London Review of Books* 38(3). https://www.lrb.co.uk/the-paper/v38/n03/ed-miliband/the-inequality-problem.

Miliband, E. 2021a. "Go big: an interview with Ed Miliband". A World To Win podcast, *Tribune*, 22 July. https://tribunemag.co.uk/2021/07/45-go-big-an-interview-with-ed-miliband.

Miliband, E. 2021b. *Go Big: How to Fix Our World*. London: Bodley Head.

Miliband, E. 2023. "Consistent and clear climate leadership". Speech to the Green Alliance, 29 March. https://labourlist.org/2023/03/consistent-and-clear-climate-leadership-milibands-speech-to-the-green-alliance/.

Miliband, R. 1972. *Parliamentary Socialism*. Pontypool: Merlin Press.

Miliband, R. 2015. *Class War Conservatism and Other Essays*. London: Verso.

Minkin, L. 2014. *The Blair Supremacy*. Manchester: Manchester University Press.

Mishra, P. 2016. "Welcome to the age of anger". *The Guardian*, 8 December. https://www.theguardian.com/politics/2016/dec/08/welcome-age-anger-brexit-trump.

Moffitt, B. 2020. *Populism*. Cambridge: Polity.

Mouffe, C. 2022. *Towards a Green Democratic Revolution*. London: Verso.

Müller, J. 2017. *What Is Populism?* London: Penguin.

Murphy, C. 2023a. *Futures of Socialism*. Cambridge: Cambridge University Press.

Murphy, C. 2023b. "The supply side and social democracy: an old story with new themes". *Renewal* 31(2): 76–82.

Murray, A. 2019. *The Fall and Rise of the British Left*. London: Verso.

Nandy, L. 2022. *All in*. Manchester: Harper North.

Nandy, L. 2023. "Tilt the balance of power back to people: Lisa Nandy MP in conversation with Karl Pike". *Renewal* 31(2): 16–23.

Nunns, A. 2018. *The Candidate*. London: OR Books.

Nutt, K. 2023. "Poll: SNP face defeat by Labour at next general election". *The Herald*, 18 June. https://www.heraldscotland.com/politics/23596592.poll-snp-face-defeat-labour-next-general-election/.

Owen, G. & D. Hodges 2023. "Labour's child sex abuser attack ad on Rishi Sunak was sparked after Keir Starmer was called 'Sir Softy' on crime". *Daily Mail*, 8 April.

Panitch, L. & C. Leys 2020. *Searching for Socialism: The Project of the Labour New Left from Benn to Corbyn*. London: Verso.

Parker, G. 2021. "Starmer urges Labour to embrace Blair's legacy as he vows to win next election". *Financial Times*, 5 August. https://www.ft.com/content/34ec43b9-5dcd-46cd-b284-093e8f13714d.

Parkin, F. 1968. *Middle Class Radicalism*. New York: Praeger.

Payne, S. 2021. *Broken Heartlands: A Journey through Labour's Lost England*. London: Macmillan.

Peston, R. 2015. "'Corbynomics' Thatcher moment". BBC News. https://www.bbc.co.uk/news/business-34376085.

Pidcock, L. 2019. "It's time to talk about class". *Tribune*, 1 November. https://tribunemag.co.uk/2019/11/its-time-to-talk-about-class.

Pike, K. 2019. "The party has a life of its own: Labour's ethos and party modernisation, 1983–1997". Unpublished PhD thesis, Queen Mary University of London.

Pike, K. 2021. "'A life of their own'? Traditions, power and 'as if realism' in political analysis". *Political Studies* 69(3): 709–24.

Pike, K. & P. Diamond 2020. "'Better in kung fu movies than in political parties': Labour's factionalism and a reappraisal of Eric Hobsbawm's political thought". *Political Quarterly* 91(4): 762–9.

Pike, K. & P. Diamond 2021. "Myth and meaning: 'Corbynism' and the interpretation of political leadership". *British Journal of Politics and International Relations* 23(4): 663–79.

Pike, K. & A. Hindmoor 2020. "Do as I did not as I say: Blair, New Labour and party traditions". *Political Quarterly* 91(1): 148–55.

Piketty, T. 2017. *Capital in the Twenty-First Century*. Cambridge, MA: Harvard University Press.

Piketty, T. 2020. *Capital and Ideology*. Cambridge, MA: Harvard University Press.

Piromalli, E. 2020. "Does socialism need fraternity? On Axel Honneth's *The Idea of Socialism*". *European Journal of Political Theory* 19(3): 375–95.

Plant, R. 1984. *Fabian Tract 494: Equality, Markets and the State*. London: Fabian Society.

Plant, R. 2004. "Ends, means and political identity". In R. Plant, M. Beech & K. Hickson (eds), *The Struggle for Labour's Soul*, 105–19. London: Routledge.

Pogrund, G. & P. Maguire 2020. *Left out*. London: Bodley Head.

Przeworski A. 1985. *Capitalism and Social Democracy*. Cambridge: Cambridge University Press.

Reeves, R. 2021. Speech to 2021 Labour Party Conference. https://labour.org.uk/press/conference-speech-rachel-reeves%E2%80%AFmp%E2%80%AF-labours%E2%80%AFshadow-chancellor-of-the-exchequer/.

Reeves, R. 2023. *A New Business Model for Britain*. London: Labour Together.

Robinson, N. 2015. *Election Notebook*. London: Transworld.

Rodrik, D. 2023. "On productivism". Harvard University. https://drodrik.scholar.harvard.edu/publications/productivism.

Rogers, J. 2021. "Ed Miliband: 'I wish I'd been bolder'". *GQ*, 9 June. https://www.gq-magazine.co.uk/politics/article/ed-miliband-interview-2021.

Rogers, S. 2022. "Labour front benchers banned from joining picket lines amid rail strikes". Politicshome, 20 June. https://www.politicshome.com/news/article/labour-front-benchers-banned-from-picket-lines-amid-rail-strikes.

Runciman, D. 2006. *The Politics of Good Intentions*. Princeton, NJ: Princeton University Press.

Rutherford, J. 2023. "Labour's future will be conservative". *New Statesman*, 24 May. https://www.newstatesman.com/quickfire/2023/05/labour-party-future-conservative.

Sartori, G. 1987. *The Theory of Democracy Revisited*. Chatham, NJ: Chatham House.

Savage, M. 2017. "Politics and the new sociology of class: a response to *The New Politics of Class* by Geoffrey Evans and James Tilley". *Political Quarterly* 88(4): 707–09.

Savage, M. 2021. *The Return of Inequality*. Cambridge, MA: Harvard University Press.

Schneider, J. 2022. *Our Bloc: How We Win*. London: Verso.

Sen, A. & B. Williams 1982. "Introduction: utilitarianism and beyond". In A. Sen & B. Williams (eds), *Utilitarianism and beyond*, 1–21. Cambridge: Cambridge University Press.

Sennett, R. 2013. *Together*. London: Penguin.

Seyd, P. & P. Whiteley 2002. *New Labour's Grassroots: The Transformation of the Labour Party Membership*. Basingstoke: Palgrave Macmillan.

Seymour, R. 2016. *Corbyn: The Strange Rebirth of Radical Politics*. London: Verso.

Shaw, E. 2004. "Labourism". In R. Plant, M. Beech & K. Hickson (eds), *The Struggle for Labour's Soul*, 187–205. London: Routledge.

Sheen, M. 2015. Transcript of speech at St David's Day event, Tredegar. https://www.theguardian.com/culture/2015/mar/02/full-text-of-michael-sheens-speech.

Shrimsley, R. 2023. "Tony Blair's unfinished business with Britain". *Financial Times*, 21 June. https://www.ft.com/content/a11e085f-0927-4b51-bdf7-4db23fac0f76.

Smart, J. & B. Williams 1973. *Utilitarianism for and against*. Cambridge: Cambridge University Press.

Sobolewska, M. & R. Ford 2020. *Brexitland*. Cambridge: Cambridge University Press.

Stacey, K. 2012. "Osborne pulls off welfare masterstroke". *Financial Times*, 5 December. https://www.ft.com/content/aa7021ea-3ee8-11e2-a095-00144feabdc0.

Stacey, K. & R. Mason 2023. "Labour rules out universal childcare for young children in fiscal credibility drive". *The Guardian*, 13 June. https://www.theguardian.com/politics/2023/jun/13/labour-rules-out-universal-childcare-for-young-children-in-fiscal-credibility-drive.

Stanley, L. 2022. *Britain Alone*. Manchester: Manchester University Press.

Starmer, K. 2020. "Labour can win again if we make the moral case for socialism". *The Guardian*, 15 January. https://www.theguardian.com/commentisfree/2020/jan/15/labour-socialism-values-election-economic-model.

Starmer, K. 2021a. "A new chapter for Britain". Labour.org, 18 February. https://labour. org.uk/a-new-chapter/.

Starmer, K. 2021b. *The Road Ahead*. London: Fabian Society. https://fabians.org.uk/wp-content/uploads/2021/09/The-Road-Ahead-KEIR-STARMER_web.pdf.

Starmer, K. 2021c. Speech to 2021 Labour Party conference. https://labour.org.uk/press/conference-speech-keir-starmer/.

Starmer, K. 2022. Speech to 2022 Labour Party Conference. https://labour.org.uk/press/keir-starmer-conference-speech/.

Starmer, K. 2023a. "Keir Starmer New Year's speech". 5 January. https://labour.org.uk/press/keir-starmer-new-years-speech/.

Starmer, K. 2023b. "Keir Starmer: my Labour is patriotic, a party of equality not protest". *The Times*, 14 February.

Starmer, K. 2023c. "Why not Britain? From sticking plaster politics to mission-driven government". Speech in Manchester, 23 February.

Starmer, K. 2023d. "Keir Starmer: this is what I believe". *New Statesman*, 1 March. https://www.newstatesman.com/politics/preparing-for-power/2023/03/keir-starmer-essay-labour-mission-what-believe.

Starmer, K. 2023e. "Sir Keir Starmer: Rishi Sunak and the Tories have let criminals get away with it … I stand by every word Labour has said, no matter how squeamish they may feel". *Daily Mail*, 9 April. https://www.dailymail.co.uk/news/article-11955043/SIR-KEIR-STARMER-Rishi-Sunak-Tories-let-criminals-away-it.html.

Starmer, K. 2023f. "Transcript: an interview with Sir Keir Starmer". *The Economist*, 26 April.

Starmer, K. 2023g. Interview on BBC *Today* programme, 2 May.

Starmer, K. 2023h. Speech to Progressive Britain Conference 2023, 13 May. https://www.youtube.com/watch?v=ocm3mRqZKxo.

Starmer, K. 2023i. Climate Mission speech, 19 June. https://labour.org.uk/press/keir-starmer-speech-unveiling-labours-mission-to-cut-bills-create-jobs-and-provide-energy-security-for-britain/.

Starmer Leadership Campaign 2020. "My pledges to you". https://keirstarmer.com/plans/10-pledges/.

Stears, M. 2011. "Democracy, leadership and organising". In M. Glasman *et al.* (eds), *The Labour Tradition and the Politics of Paradox*, 57–71. Oxford London Seminars/Soundings. https://static1.squarespace.com/static/5d1890f32eb7e50001d7bb7f/t/6292447f74726d213fe76114/1653752961593/Labour_tradition_and_the_politics_of_paradox.pdf.

Steers, A. 2021. "The media's love affair with New Labour". *Tribune*, 25 October. https://tribunemag.co.uk/2021/10/tony-blair-gordon-brown-new-labour-documentary-review.

Stewart, H. & L. O'Carroll 2018. "Labour delegates back Keir Starmer push for public vote on Brexit". *The Guardian*, 25 September. https://www.theguardian.com/politics/2018/sep/25/labour-delegates-back-keir-starmer-push-for-public-vote-on-brexit.

Stone, J. 2016. "Liz Kendall says she lost the Labour leadership election because she was the 'eat your greens' candidate". *The Independent*, 26 January. https://www.

independent.co.uk/news/uk/politics/liz-kendall-says-she-lost-the-labour-leadership-election-because-she-was-the-eat-your-greens-candidate-a6835011.html.

Stratton, A. 2011a. "Ed and David Miliband shake hands on plan for 'army' of 10,000 activists". *The Guardian*, 25 January. https://www.theguardian.com/politics/2011/jan/25/ed-david-miliband-activists.

Stratton, A. 2011b. "Playing the long game: Ed Miliband shuns quick fixes in first 100 days". *The Guardian*, 3 January. https://www.theguardian.com/politics/2011/jan/03/ed-miliband-first-100-days.

Stratton, A. & P. Wintour 2010. "Ed Miliband: 'We're brothers, not clones. I'm different from David'". *The Guardian*, 21 May. https://www.theguardian.com/politics/2010/may/21/ed-miliband-interview.

Streeting, W. 2023. Tonight with Andrew Marr. LBC, 23 February. https://www.lbc.co.uk/radio/presenters/andrew-marr/tonight-with-andrew-marr-23-02-watch-again/.

Sullivan, J. 2023. "Remarks by National Security Advisor Jake Sullivan on renewing American economic leadership at the Brookings Institution". 27 April. https://www.whitehouse.gov/briefing-room/speeches-remarks/2023/04/27/remarks-by-national-security-advisor-jake-sullivan-on-renewing-american-economic-leadership-at-the-brookings-institution/.

Sultana, Z. 2021. "As a former community organiser, here's why Labour should keep the unit". LabourList, 15 February. https://labourlist.org/2021/02/as-a-former-community-organiser-heres-why-labour-should-keep-the-unit/.

Sweney, M. 2015. "Ed Miliband's Question Time grilling dominates headlines – except the Mail". *The Guardian*, 1 May. https://www.theguardian.com/media/2015/may/01/ed-miliband-question-time-slip-mail-election-debate.

Taylor, C. 2022. "Degenerations of democracy". In C. Calhoun, D. Gaonkar & C. Taylor (eds), *Degenerations of Democracy*, 18–47. Cambridge, MA: Harvard University Press.

The Voice Newspaper 2020. "Keir Starmer talks to The Voice about Black Lives Matter 'moment' comment and police funding". YouTube. https://www.youtube.com/watch?v=AlsRaYOF3Bk.

Thompson, P. 2016. "Corbynism isn't a social movement, and Labour shouldn't be one". *Renewal* blog, 24 August. https://renewal.org.uk/corbynism-isnt-a-social-movement-and-labour-shouldnt-be-one/.

Toynbee, P. 2010. "Labour's vain, venal has-beens should bow out and shut up". *The Guardian*, 30 August. https://www.theguardian.com/commentisfree/2010/aug/30/vain-venal-has-beens-mandelson.

Toynbee, P. 2018. "The NHS is our religion: it's the only thing that saves it from the Tories". *The Guardian*, 3 July. https://www.theguardian.com/commentisfree/2018/jul/03/nhs-religion-tories-health-service.

Toynbee, P. 2019. "Jeremy Corbyn has to get off the fence for Labour to see off the Faragists". *The Guardian*, 13 May. https://www.theguardian.com/commentisfree/2019/may/13/jeremy-corbyn-labour-brexit-nigel-farage-european-elections.

Toynbee, P. 2023. "This is Starmer's moment: Thatcherism has collapsed, and the Tories are at each other's throats". *The Guardian*, 12 June. https://www.theguardian.

com/commentisfree/2023/jun/12/keir-starmer-moment-thatcherism-collapsed-tories-existential-crisis.

Van Kessel, S. 2014. "The populist cat-dog: applying the concept of populism to contemporary European party systems". *Journal of Political Ideologies* 19(1): 99–108.

Wainwright, H. 2016. "The making of Jeremy Corbyn". *Jacobin*, 3 September. https://jacobin.com/2016/03/tony-benn-corbyn-thatcher-labour-leadership.

Walker, P., J. Elgot & R. Mason 2017. "Labour conference votes to back party's official policy on Brexit". *The Guardian*, 25 September. https://www.theguardian.com/politics/2017/sep/25/john-mcdonnell-labour-members-didnt-want-to-split-party-on-brexit.

Walker, P., H. Stewart & J. Elgot 2018. "McDonnell: new Brexit referendum should not include remain option". *The Guardian*, 24 September. https://www.theguardian.com/politics/2018/sep/24/mcdonnell-new-brexit-referendum-should-not-include-remain-option.

Walker P., R. Syal & H. Stewart 2019. "Labour's free broadband plan fires up the election battle". *The Guardian*, 15 November. https://www.theguardian.com/technology/2019/nov/15/free-broadband-essential-uk-compete-john-mcdonnell-labour-policy-openreach.

Watson, T. 2019. "The future of Britain and Europe". Speech to the Centre for European Reform, 17 June. https://www.cer.eu/sites/default/files/speech_tomwatson_cer_17.6.19.pdf.

Watts, J. & T. Bale 2019. "Populism as an intra-party phenomenon: the British Labour Party under Jeremy Corbyn". *British Journal of Politics and International Relations* 21(1): 99–115.

Waugh, P. 2016. "Jeremy Corbyn hits back at Tony Blair's 'politics of protest' attack". Huffington Post, 8 June. https://www.huffingtonpost.co.uk/entry/jeremy-corbyn-tony-blair-politics-of-protest-bloomberg_uk_5758129fe4b014b4f2530c76.

Wearmouth, R. 2022. "Keir Starmer: 'Am I aiming to be just a one-term prime minister? No, of course not'". *New Statesman*, 7 December. https://www.newstatesman.com/preparing-for-power/2022/12/keir-starmer-interview-prime-minister-labour-leader.

Webb, P. & T. Bale 2017. "No place else to go". In A. Haugsgjerd & T. Bale (eds), *Left-of-Centre Parties and Trade Unions in the Twenty-First Century*, 246–63. Oxford: Oxford University Press.

White House 2022. "President's budget rewards work, not wealth with new billionaire minimum income tax". White House briefing, 28 March. https://www.whitehouse.gov/omb/briefing-room/2022/03/28/presidents-budget-rewards-work-not-wealth-with-new-billionaire-minimum-income-tax/.

White, J. & L. Ypi 2016. "The new partisanship". *Renewal* 24(2): 27–35.

Whiteley, P. *et al.* 2019. "Oh Jeremy Corbyn! Why did Labour Party membership soar after the 2015 general election?" *British Journal of Politics and International Relations* 21(1): 80–98.

Wickham-Jones, M. 2021. "Neoliberalism and the Labour Party". In A. Davies, B. Jackson & F. Sutcliffe-Braithwaite (eds), *The Neoliberal Age? Britain since the 1970s*, 226–53. London: UCL Press.

Williams, B. 1981. *Moral Luck*. Cambridge: Cambridge University Press.

Williams, S. 1981. *Politics Is for People*. Harmondsworth: Penguin.

Williams, Z. & H. Stewart 2019. "Keir Starmer sets out case for 'radical Labour government'". *The Guardian*, 18 December. https://www.theguardian.com/politics/2019/dec/17/keir-starmer-labour-leadership-pitch-radical-government.

Wintour, P. 2010. "David Miliband under fire for lukewarm Gordon Brown backing". *The Guardian*, 7 January. https://www.theguardian.com/politics/2010/jan/07/david-miliband-gordon-brown-labour.

Wintour, P. 2011a. "Andy Coulson resigns as No 10 director of communications". *The Guardian*, 21 January. https://www.theguardian.com/media/2011/jan/21/andy-coulson-resigns.

Wintour, P. 2011b. "Blue Labour guru Glasman apologies over immigration remarks". *The Guardian*, 21 July. https://www.theguardian.com/uk/2011/jul/21/lord-glasman-apologises-immigration-remarks.

Wintour, P. & A. Stratton 2010. "Ed Miliband: Labour's catastrophic loss of trust over Iraq". *The Guardian*, 21 May. https://www.theguardian.com/politics/2010/may/21/ed-miliband-labour-iraq-war.

Wolf, M. 2023. *The Crisis of Democratic Capitalism*. London: Allen Lane.

YouGov 2019. Conservative Party Members Poll. https://d25d2506sfb94s.cloudfront.net/cumulus_uploads/document/mxtlaay6zu/YouGov%20-%20Conservative%20members%20poll%20190614.pdf.

YouGov 2021. Labour Party Members Poll. https://docs.cdn.yougov.com/q8hebbhxm4/Internal_LabMembers_Results_W.pdf.

Zeffman, H. 2023. "Keir Starmer: I will be ruthless in pursuit of power". *The Times*, 3 April. https://www.thetimes.co.uk/article/keir-starmer-i-will-be-ruthless-in-pursuit-of-power-b7v606rg7.

INDEX